MW00776305

Aristophanes' Male and Female Revolutions

APPLICATIONS OF POLITICAL THEORY

Series Editors: Harvey C. Mansfield, Harvard University, and Daniel J. Mahoney, Assumption College

This series encourages analysis of the applications of political theory to various domains of thought and action. Such analysis will include works on political thought and literature, statesmanship, American political thought, and contemporary political theory. The editors also anticipate and welcome examinations of the place of religion in public life and commentary on classic works of political philosophy.

Gladly to Learn and Gladly to Teach: Essays on Religion and Political Philosophy in Honor of Ernest L. Fortin, A.A., edited and introduced by Michael P. Foley and Douglas Kries

Dissent and Philosophy in the Middle Ages: Dante and His Precursors, by Ernest L. Fortin; translated by Marc A. LePain

Behemoth *Teaches* Leviathan: *Thomas Hobbes on Political Education*, by Geoffrey M. Vaughan

The Dialogue in Hell between Machiavelli and Montesquieu: Humanitarian Despotism and the Conditions of Modern Tyranny, by Maurice Joly; edited and translated by John S. Waggoner

Cultivating Citizens: Soulcraft and Citizenship in Contemporary America, edited by Dwight D. Allman and Michael D. Beaty

Liberty, Wisdom, and Grace: Thomism and Democratic Political Theory, by John P. Hittinger

The Paradox of Philosophical Education: Nietzsche's New Nobility and the Eternal Recurrence in Beyond Good and Evil, by J. Harvey Lomax

Faith, Morality, and Civil Society, edited by Dale McConkey and Peter Augustine Lawler

History of American Political Thought, edited by Bryan-Paul Frost and Jeffrey Sikkenga

Totalitarianism and the Prospects for World Order: Closing the Door on the Twentieth Century, by Aleksandras Shtromas; and edited by Daniel J. Mahoney and Robert Faulkner

Liberalism under Siege: The Political Thought of the French Doctrinaires, by Aurelian Craiutu

Assault on Ideology, second edition, by James F. Pontuso

The Deconstitutionalization of America: The Forgotten Frailties of Democratic Rule, by Roger M. Barrus, John H. Eastby, Joseph H. Lane Jr., David E. Marion, and James F. Pontuso

Plato's Cleitophon: *On Socrates and the Modern Mind,* edited, introduced, and translated by Mark Kremer

Uncivil Society: The Perils of Pluralism and the Making of Modern Liberalism, by Richard Boyd

Aristophanes' Male and Female Revolutions: A Reading of Aristophanes' Knights *and* Assemblywomen, by Kenneth M. De Luca

Breaking with Athens: Alfarabi as Founder, by Christopher A. Colmo

Aristophanes' Male and Female Revolutions

A Reading of Aristophanes' Knights *and* Assemblywomen

Kenneth M. De Luca

LEXINGTON BOOKS
Lanham • Boulder • New York • Toronto • Oxford

LEXINGTON BOOKS

Published in the United States of America
by Lexington Books
An imprint of The Rowman & Littlefield Publishing Group, Inc.
4501 Forbes Boulevard, Suite 200, Lanham, Maryland 20706

PO Box 317
Oxford
OX2 9RU, UK

British Library Cataloguing in Publication Information Available
Library of Congress Cataloging-in-Publication Data

De Luca, Kenneth M.
Aristophanes' male and female revolutions : a reading of Aristophanes' Knights and Assemblywomen / Kenneth M. De Luca.
p. cm.
Includes bibliographical references and index.
ISBN 0-7391-0833-6 (pbk. : alk. paper)
1. Aristophanes. Knights. 2. Aristophanes—Characters—Men. 3. Aristophanes. Ecclesiazusae. 4. Political plays, Greek—History and criticism. 5. Aristophanes—Characters—Women. 6. Politics and literature—Greece. 7. Women and literature—Greece. 8. Sex role in literature. 9. Women in literature. 10. Men in literature. 11. Comedy. I. Title. II. Series.
PA3875.E73 D425 2004
882'.01 22 2004017684

Printed in the United States of America

∞™ The paper used in this publication meets the minimum requirements of American National Standard for Information Sciences—Permanence of Paper for Printed Library Materials, ANSI/NISO Z39.48–1992.

For my parents,
Tom and Patricia

CONTENTS

ACKNOWLEDGEMENTS

Mary Nichols provided innumerable thoughtful comments so many of which have been incorporated that all I can do is admit that without her help this book would never have seen the light of day. Seth Benardete's probing questions and remarks contributed greatly to my understanding of both the *Knights* and the *Assemblywomen*. He also corrected my translation of excerpts from the *Knights*. Michael Davis' insights on both the *Knights* and the *Assemblywomen* and on Greek poetry and philosophy were invaluable. This book also owes its existence to the encouragement, advice and understanding of Daniel Mahoney and David Schaefer. Jon Marken did an excellent job setting the text. The Earhart Foundation provided a grant that facilitated the completion of the book.

INTRODUCTION

In this book I provide interpretations of two plays of the Ancient Greek comic playwright Aristophanes—the *Knights* and the *Assemblywomen.* Why Aristophanes? Aristophanes' comedy begins with the particular, with Athens—its politicians, politics, poetry and philosophy—and ascends to the universal. He starts with what is true for his time and ends up showing us what is true everywhere.[1] Thus, in the *Clouds* Aristophanes puts the philosopher of his time, Socrates, on stage and teaches us about philosophy. In the *Knights* and the *Assemblywomen*, he puts his regime on the stage and teaches us about democracy, our regime.

Why these two plays? Both plays are about democracy, and both present democratic revolutions, but the democracy and the revolution each presents are radically different. In the *Knights*, the revolution is set in historical Athens, while in the *Assemblywomen*, the revolution abstracts from contemporary circumstance. In the *Knights*, Aristophanes puts the reigning demagogue Cleon on the stage (named, in the play, Paphlagon),[2] while in the *Assemblywomen*, the action of the play is not driven by any known historical figure. As their titles suggest, the *Assemblywomen* is more a thought experiment.[3] The revolution of the *Knights* is much more contentious than that of the *Assemblywomen.* The contest for power which the *Knights* features between Cleon and a man recruited from off the street consumes almost the entire play (274-1260), and is waged with numerous insults, indictments, threats, curses and even physical violence. By contrast, the revolution of the *Assemblywomen* is decided in the first third of the play, and is fought off stage. The audience is not even permitted to view it. Thus, the *Knights* accentuates conflict, while the *Assemblywomen* suppresses it. The action of the *Knights* is entirely driven by the question of who will rule Athens. In the *Assemblywomen*, the question of rule is deemphasized. Praxagora, the female architect of Athens' new regime and its new ruler, leaves the stage at line 724, and never returns.[4] In the *Assemblywomen*, the controversy is not so much over who, but over the type of rule Athens should have.[5] That is, the controversy here is not about rule but about the law—the conventions that ought to govern the city.[6] These differences between the plays, in turn, are related to another obvious difference. Whereas the *Knights* features mostly men, the *Assemblywomen* features women.

Thus, like male and female, the plays could not be more different and they could not be more the same. One might say of our two plays what Rousseau says of the two genders: "From this double perspective, we find them [male and female] related in so many ways and opposed in so many other ways that it is perhaps one of the marvels of nature to have been able to construct two such similar beings who are constituted so differently."[7] Like man and woman, both plays are not only different but in important ways opposing. Moreover, their opposition can be cast in terms of gender. In the *Knights*, women do not even appear until line 1388, whereas in the *Assemblywomen* men appear but are feckless. Accordingly, both plays trumpet different virtues. The *Knights* idealizes courage. There are several glowing references to it.[8] Whereas the *Assemblywomen*, less obviously than the *Knights* with respect to courage, idealizes moderation.[9]

The *Knights* and the *Assemblywomen*[10] seem to form two halves of a whole. They complete one another, and yet are in tension with one another. Are the tensions between them as revealing of and fundamental to democracy, as the tensions between male and female are revealing and fundamental to human life?

Although we will be, hopefully, in a better position to understand this question after studying these plays, a few things can be said at the outset.

Every political regime blends what the cities of the *Knights* and the *Assemblywomen* treat as separable—rule, or active intelligence,[11] and the law. The one without the other, regardless of which, seems to land a regime on the same rocky shoal. If rule is not supported by the law, by principle, then rule is purely the manifestation of the will of the one who rules. If the law is not supported by rule, by an active intelligence, then inevitably the law will be applied to a circumstance which was not contemplated at the time of its formulation. Whether a regime commits the first mistake or the second, the result seems the same—arbitrary government, or tyranny. Aristophanes' two plays suggest that despite the disaster that awaits the regime that dares to simplify its government by embracing only one of these two necessary elements, there is something about democracy which inclines it in the direction of disaster. Despite the need for both rule and the law, because rule and the law are supported by conflicting rationales, regimes, especially democratic regimes, are tempted to exclude one or the other.

In a democracy, the people rule. So, what need is there for law? The demos makes the easy assumption that its will can be translated into action with nothing getting lost in translation. The demos believes that public servants are mere executors of its will.[12] On this view, the law, written or not, stands in the way of perfected democracy. The *Knights* is the absurd representation of this absurd but seemingly logical claim.

While democracy means the people rule, what next? What does the people do with its power? What is the end towards which democracy should aim? The *Assemblywomen* takes up this line of argument. Democracy is founded upon the idea that no one or no class of people deserves to lord it over others. Equality justifies the rule of the people. However, equality justifies only because equality is regarded as just. So in formulating laws, it is not surprising that equality is the standard towards which democratic law aims. However servile are public servants, given the fixity of the principle which underlies democracy, what need is there for human superintendence? Moreover, despite the myth of the *Knights*, public servants are never just servants. Unlike the law, they impose their will and they err. Democracy calls for a government of laws not men. The *Assemblywomen* is the absurd representation of this absurd but seemingly logical claim.

One might ask, why do we need Aristophanes' *Knights* and *Assemblywomen* if all they do is to prove that claims virtually no one makes are absurd? Moreover, even if we were in need of such a proof, would we not be better off looking for it in authors who speak in a more accessible tongue than does Aristophanes, such as Tocqueville, Publius and countless contemporary political scientists? Furthermore, how can Aristophanes' old medicine have therapeutic value for us very modern men?

The practical value of reading Aristophanes' plays lies not in specific policy recommendations which emerge from them but from the understanding they yield about rule and law in a democratic regime. Just because few advocate direct democracy or the absolute superintendance of law does not mean that we are unaffected by the arguments which underlie these extremes. For the arguments can do damage even if they manifest themselves in something short of an extreme. By making us laugh at these extremes, Aristophanes also makes us laugh at the arguments which underlie them, and so Aristophanes induces us to question their validity. One can induce such questioning in a prose argument, but which is more likely to arouse suspicions in a democratic populace (or even in a philosopher) of the errors of egalitarianism, Milton Friedman's *Capitalism and Freedom*, or the hag scene of Aristophanes' *Assemblywomen*? Which is more likely to arouse suspicion of a Ross Perot and his attempt to position himself as a mere spokesman of the demos[13] by pushing "the electronic town hall meeting," Publius' arguments or the hysterical sausage-seller of Aristophanes' *Knights*?

In response to my claim that Aristophanes' comedy has the ability to greatly influence ordinary people (i.e., those who rule in a democracy), one might ask, Cannot philosophy be just as, if not more influential? This seems to depend on the philosopher. Not all philosophers have sought to influence ordinary people. Those that have have produced highly questionable results. Consider, for example, Rousseau and Marx. It is obvious that both intended to affect mass opinion. And, both did. To the extent that Rousseau contributed to the French Revolution and Marx to various twentieth-century revolutions, it seems to me that Aristophanes as a teacher of the people does well by comparison. Rousseau's and Marx's writings drive democracy towards the extremes. By contrast, Aristophanes' *Knights* and *Assemblywomen* serve to moderate democracy. Since democracy is prone towards the extremes given its basis in an idea, idealist philosophers such as Rousseau and Marx may certainly be influential, but whether their influence is healthy is subject to question. In comparison with Rousseau and Marx, and even the Federalist, Aristophanes' comedy functions like a Platonic dialogue, in that when read properly it attempts to lead us away from extremes. It generates doubt by depicting things we might take too seriously in a comic way.

Reforming a people's understanding, leading them away from the extremes, is always a matter of contingency, but it is hard to imagine a more effective way of doing so than Aristophanes' comedy. For the absurdity of an Aristophanic image is immediately recognized as such even if the reason for its being absurd is not. Moreover, the exercise of following a play, of watching or imagining the action unfold affects us in a way that it is very difficult for a prose argument to match. For the story transports us into the situation of the drama and changes us whether we like it or not. As the Greeks said, *pathei mathos*, learning comes through suffering, or through experience. Laughter is the suffering of comedy, or is a sign that we are experiencing the comedy.[14] Once we experience it, it is hard to flush the experience and everything associated with it from our thinking. According to Plato's *Apology,* Aristophanes' depiction of Socrates unalterably changed the public's perception of him, although in this case I doubt that Aristophanes was happy about it.[15] What I have tried to do in this book is delve into the *Knights* and the *Assemblywomen*, to think them through in order to provide a rational account of their absurdity, or why they strike us as funny. For while there is no denying the immediacy of Aristophanic humor, as the case of the *Clouds* shows, unless we reflect upon Aristophanes' plays, we cannot be sure we get the joke.

In part I, I address the *Knights*; in part II, I address the *Assemblywomen*; and in the conclusion, I explore the connection between them. Parts I and II are further divided into chapters.

In my treatment of the *Knights*, taking my lead from the play itself, I closely follow the plot. Why does the action of the *Knights* take the course it does? This question the play itself prompts us to ask. For the plot seems to move along without rhyme or reason. In the *Knights* almost everything appears accidental. It appears as though things could have happened otherwise. However, if Aristophanes is a poet worthy of his reputation and of the attention of Plato, nothing could have happened otherwise. Everything that happens happens by necessity, or is determined by the point that Aristophanes is trying to make. To get at this point, just as one would do when analyzing an event, I pay close attention to the plot or to the action.

In each chapter, I provide separate treatments of a different episode, and I do not contemplate the whole until the end. In the *Knights* we are continuously reflecting on parts, and always wondering how the parts fit together or what the whole means. The challenge one faces in attempting to understand the *Knights* is not unlike the challenge one faces in attempting to understand an historical event.[16] This perhaps is not surprising for as mentioned above the play is set in historical Athens.[17] Is what happens in the play or in an historical event necessary, or accidental? If necessary, then one can derive a teaching from it; if accidental, then perfectly particular, and therefore unintelligible or non-generalizable, and one cannot derive a teaching from it.

Chapter 1 analyzes the opening of the play and attempts to explain the ciphers that Aristophanes employs: Demos stands for the people, *oikos* for the city, slaves for the politicians, and Paphlagon for Cleon. This chapter sets up the theme that I suggest runs through the play, the collapsing of the public and the private. Chapter 2 examines Demosthenes' rationale for recruiting as his hero and Paphlagon's adversary the first sausage-seller from off the street. This rationale offers us a glimpse of his view of extreme democracy, a view which the sausage-seller will eventually correct. In chapter 3, I reflect upon the meaning of the sausage-seller's longest speech, his account of his Senate victory over Paphlagon. This chapter allows us to draw a contrast between Paphlagon and the sausage-seller, and through it we begin to see why the move from Paphlagon to the sausage-seller should be characterized as a descent. In chapter 4, I interpret the love speeches Paphlagon and the sausage-seller offer Demos. A love speech is an attempt to attract a beloved's love by clothing oneself in an image a beloved will find beautiful. Thus, it tells as much about the lover as it does the beloved. It reveals what the lover regards as lovable. Thus, this scene enables us to understand the competing ideals of Paphlagon and the sausage-seller, and what it means that the sausage-seller is the one Demos falls for. In chapter 5, I look at the remainder of the play, showing how the interpretation of the first half of the play provided in chapters 1-4 sheds light on the play's conclusion. In this chapter, I explain the significance of the sausage-seller's victory over Paphlagon, of his returning old man Demos to youth and of his presentation of the Spartan peace terms, personified as prostitutes, to Demos. In victory, the sausage-seller brings about Demos' thorough privatization. This chapter delves into the connection between this eventuality and democracy.[18]

In part II, I offer my reading of the *Assemblywomen*. In chapter 6, I delve into Praxagora's soliloquy which opens the play and within which she pays homage to her lamp. In chapter 7, I interpret her rehearsal speech. In chapter 8, I explain the significance of her reform program. In chapter 9, I analyze the famous "hag scene." And, in chapter 10, I attempt to show how the play as a whole satires democratic egalitarianism.

Just about everyone who has intelligently read the *Assemblywomen* has drawn a comparison between it and Book V of Plato's *Republic*, and vice versa.[19]

I treat this fact as reflective of the philosophic depth of the play, and attempt to draw it out. The *Assemblywomen* has also been read as a criticism of egalitarian extremism.[20] While offering my own version of this criticism, my interpretation of the *Assemblywomen* is unique also in recognizing and understanding the play on both levels.[21]

Leo Strauss in his *Socrates and Aristophanes* offers interpretations of all of Aristophanes' extant plays, including the *Knights* and the *Assemblywomen*. Having read his brilliant interpretations at the start of my research, in order to learn for myself what these two plays are about, I have shielded my eyes from them as my research proceeded. The differences that have emerged between our analyses are mostly due to emphasis. For example, in the *Knights*, I offer a close reading of two scenes: the sausage-seller's account of his victory in the Senate, and the first part of his debate with Paphlagon in the Assembly, both of which point towards the sausage-seller's move towards privatizing the city, and what this privatization means. Strauss does not give these two scenes the consideration I do, and so his interpretation does not push the idea of privatization and its connection to democracy as far as mine does. In the *Assemblywomen*, to offer an example regarding this play, I explain the significance of Praxagora's opening soliloquy, which I argue points towards Praxagora's faith in techne, a theme I regard as crucial to understanding the *Assemblywomen*. Strauss regards Praxagora's speech as remarkable and therefore worthy of serious consideration, but he does not have much more to say about it. I also offer a line by line interpretation of the hag scene, which makes clear the conflict between the rule of law and spiritedness, and explains the ugliness of the scene. Strauss calls this scene the ugliest in all of Aristophanic comedy. While my analysis focuses on aspects of the hag scene which Strauss either ignores or downplays, my interpretation of the scene supports Strauss' conclusion.

Notes

1. Greek tragedy begins with the universal. Its main characters usually are gods and/or mythic figures—beings with universal meaning. Unlike Aristophanes' comedy, Greek tragedy usually abstracts from contemporary circumstances and personages. In Greek tragedy, one is hardly aware of the people. In the *Knights*, "The People" is a main character. "Aristophanes regularly represents the comic poet and the comic hero as people of ordinary or even rather low status. . . . This factor was perhaps enhanced in Athens by a deliberate desire to define comedy as different from its more august older sibling, tragedy." A.M. Bowie, *Aristophanes: Myth, Ritual and Comedy* (Cambridge: Cambridge University Press, 1993): 13. Cf. Oliver Taplin, "Fifth Century Tragedy and Comedy" in Erich Segal, ed., *Oxford Readings in Aristophanes* (Oxford: Oxford University Press, 1996), 162-81;

Seth Benardete, "On Greek Tragedy," in *Current Developments in the Arts and Sciences*, The Great Ideas Today, 1980, 102-3 (Chicago: Encyclopedia Britannica, 1980).

2. *Paphlagon* means man from Paphlagonia, in northern Asia Minor. The name mockingly suggests that Paphlagon is of barbarian descent. *Paphlagon* also sounds like the verb *Paphlazo*, which may mean to storm or bluster. In the play, Paphlagon frequently lives up to his name, as he seems to have done in life. "[The Paphlagonians] form part of a group of peoples on the Euxine coast with characteristics that mark them as separate from the Greek world." Bowie, *Aristophanes*, 59. "His name not only puns on *paphlazein*, but recalls the *kumata paphlazonta*, 'foaming waves', of Homer." Ibid., 62.

3. In Athens, there were knights, but there were no assemblywomen. Women did not freely travel in public, let alone enter the Assembly. "As their disappointed husbands point out, the women 'are not at home' they have 'gone out' (325), indeed 'sneaked out' (337). Leaving in this way, according to Blepyrus, is clearly a revolutionary infraction." Suzanne Said, "The *Assemblywomen*: Women, Economy, and Politics," in *Oxford Readings*, 1996, 291. Cf. Arlene Saxonhouse, *The Fear of Diversity* (Chicago: University of Chicago Press, 1992): 5.

4. Strauss observes that the *Assemblywomen* is unique in providing for the mid-play disappearance of the character responsible for the action. Leo Strauss, *Socrates and Aristophanes* (Chicago: University of Chicago Press, 1966): 273.

5. Although in both regimes, the revolution that comes brings about a change in the form of rule, this change is far more obvious in the *Assemblywomen*. In the *Knights*, Cleon accuses the sausage-seller of endearing himself to Demos by aping his own ways. In the *Assemblywomen*, the women ape no one. As they themselves acknowledge, their rule is a thorough-going novelty. 578-80; cf. 215-20.

Against this, Kremer and Bloom suggest that Praxagora's disappearance is self-interested. Praxagora creates a regime tailor-made to satisfy her. She creates a regime whose laws make adultery legal. Mark Kremer, "Aristophanes' Criticism of Egalitarianism: An Interpretation of the *Assemblywomen*," *Interpretation* 21, no. 3 (Spring 1994): 261-74. So, in the view of these men there is continuity between pre- and post-revolutionary Athens—in both self-interest dominates. Allan Bloom, *Giants and Dwarfs* (New York: Simon Schuster, 1990): 170-6.

6. "The society Praxagora creates depends on lawfulness, that is the priority of the law over the self." Saxonhouse, *Fear of Diversity*, 13.

7. Jean-Jacques Rousseau, *Emile*, trans. Allan Bloom (New York: Basic Books, 1979): 358.

8. *Andreia* (courage) is etymologically related to manliness (*andria*). *Andreia* appears at 268. At 368, the sausage-seller, Paphlagon's opponent, threatens to indict him for cowardice. At 390, the knights, attempting to reassure the sausage-seller, predict that Paphlagon will prove himself a coward. In the parabasis 506-610, the chorus of knights praises the courage of the poet for advancing nobly against the typhoon (Paphlagon?, 511), their ancestors for their indifference to bodily injury and self-interest (565-80) and their horses for their "manly" actions (599). At 182, the sausage-seller evidences self-restraint, if not moderation, and is quickly remonstrated for doing so (183-5).

9. *Sophron*, temperate, appears at 767. *Sophronousa*, being moderate, appears at 1038. Though it only makes three appearances, that the play is in some sense about moderation is suggested by a closer look at the word and the play, which we can but touch on here. Moderation, in Greek, *sophrosune*, combines two words: *sos*, which may mean safe, certain, and *phren*, which may mean mind, heart or understanding. The word *sos* is taken

up in the verb, *sozo*, which may mean to save, and in the noun, *soteria*, which may mean deliverance or a keeping safe. The latter word occurs at 396, the former at 402. The agenda of the assembly meeting during which Praxagora assumes control over Athens is the city's *soteria*, or preservation. As we shall show, Praxagora brings mind or reason to bear upon Athens in such a way that Athens will never need to take up the question of its preservation again. If *sophrosune* means the preservation of mind, then Praxagora's Athens perfectly embodies it.

In concluding his interpretation of the *Assemblywomen*, Strauss states that the play "reflects the ugliness of moderation." Strauss, *Socrates and Aristophanes*, 281-2.

10. About the Athens of the *Assemblywomen* Kremer says "[i]t will not be a harsh father demanding the sacrifice of comfort and life for the glory of the fatherland. She will be a kind and gentle mother providing each of her children with the necessities of life." Kremer, *Assemblywomen*, 263. Kremer not only points to the notion that the *Assemblywomen* represents the female view of democracy, but hints at the male, or harsh view, that is the *Knights*. Kremer and I both regard the *Assemblywomen* as offering profound insights into the nature of democracy and the dangers of egalitarianism, and our interpretations overlap in several places. However, unlike Kremer, I regard the *Assemblywomen* not only as a reflection on democratic egalitarianism, but also on law.

11. What I mean by rule is the rule of someone or some group, a pilot as it were. It is no accident that in investigating the phenomenon of rule within a regime philosophers employ the metaphor of the ship. In the *Republic*, in order to explain to Adeimantus what he means when he says the polis is in need of a philosopher-king, Socrates uses this metaphor. Plato, *Republic*, 487e1-489a2, trans. Allan Bloom (New York: Basic Books, 1968). Aquinas uses the same metaphor in *On Kingship* in the very opening of the book, "A ship, for example, which moves in different directions according to the impulse of the changing winds, would never reach its destination were it not brought to port by the skill of the pilot." Thomas Aquinas, *On Kingship*, 1.1.2, trans. Gerald Phelan (Toronto: The Pontifical Institute of Medieval Studies, 1949). Political life requires active intelligence, that is, a mind on the alert for changing conditions.

12. We should mention at this point that Aristophanes in the *Knights* presents the politicians as Demos' slaves.

13. Perot resembles Paphlagon in that both hail the legislative supremacy of the people. Paphlagon pays homage to the Pnyx, and Perot supports the creation of government by town hall meeting. Instead of meeting in the Assembly, citizens assemble individually in front of their computer. Perot's idea would give life to Aristophanes' poetic monster.

14. Cf. M. Croiset, *Aristophanes and the Political Parties at Athens*, trans. J. Loeb (London: Macmillan, 1909): xv. "The Instrument by which the poet probed the popular discontent was that most effective of all means when skilfully used—a laugh."

15. In Plato's *Apology*, at 18d and 19c, Socrates suggests that his being indicted is caused, in part, by Aristophanes' *Clouds*. In a queer way, Aristophanes' depiction may have kept Socrates alive for seventy years while at the same time preventing him from getting any older. For the *Clouds* in depicting Socrates unseriously suggests that in Socrates there was nothing to seriously worry about.

16. At least one interpreter was misled into treating the *Knights* as history not poetry. See Croiset, *Aristophanes*, chapter 2.

17. The backdrop of the play is the events of 425-4. Paphlagon, or Cleon, is at the peak of his power, having just returned from Pylos with the Spartan hostages, to the chagrin of

Demosthenes and Nicias, generals and rival politicians of Cleon. There is great similarity between Aristophanes' and Thucydides' accounts of the leading politicians and of the situation in Athens at this time. Thucydides, *The Peloponnesian War,* 3. 1-41, trans. Richard Crawley (London: Everyman's Library Edition, 1993).

18. As far as I know, with the exception of Leo Strauss, no one has read the *Knights* as a trenchant representation of democracy and political life. Commentators see the *Knights* either as a manifestation of his political views be they conservative, moderate or what have you. Croiset goes so far as to label Aristophanes a "pamphleteer." Croiset, *Aristophanes*, 61ff. Or they assert that Aristophanes' views are unknowable.

19. For an example of the former, see R.G. Ussher, *Aristophanes: Ecclesiazusai* (Oxford: Oxford University Press, 1973): 157, with respect to lines 590-610; Said, "The *Assemblywomen*," 282; Helene Foley, "The 'Female Intruder' Reconsidered," *Classical Philology* 77 (January 1982): 15, n.33; Casement, "Political Theory in Aristophanes' *Ecclesiazusae*," *J Thought*, 21 (Winter 1986): 76-7; and Kremer, "Aristophanes' Criticism of Egalitarianism," 261. For an example of the latter, see Allan Bloom, *The Republic of Plato* (New York: Basic Books, 1968): 381. In *Giants and Dwarfs*, Bloom provides an interesting but brief comparative analysis of the central conceit (community of women) of both the *Assemblywomen* and Book V of the *Republic*. Ussher makes the comparison, but does not delve into it.

20. See Arlene Saxonhouse, *Fear of Diversity*; "Political Theory in Aristophanes' *Ecclesiazusae*," William Casement; "Aristophanes' Criticism of Egalitarianism," Mark Kremer. They read the play as an attack on egalitarianism. "The women, by acquiring power in the city, obliterate one of the critical differences between the sexes in Athens, and having overcome that distinction, try to transcend many other divisions as well, only to discover that in so doing they introduce chaos rather than a new order to the city." Saxonhouse, *Diversity*, 1. "The emancipation of women is an exaggerated connecting thread which helps to reveal the overall and unifying political message of the play to be that democracy and communism, are bound to fail, as both derive from the same infirm root—the principle of equality." Casement, "*Ecclesiazusae*," 65. With respect to Kremer, consider the title of his essay. See also Strauss, *Socrates and Aristophanes*, 279.

21. It is also unique in juxtaposing the *Assemblywomen* and the *Knights*; however, to the say the least, I am not the first to see the two plays as worth juxtaposing. "The fundamental political predicament is disposed of in the *Knights* by the absorption of the individuals into the individual called Demos, as well as by the absence of women (and children). Aristophanes will experiment with the diametrically opposed solution in the *Assembly of Women*." Strauss, *Socrates and Aristophanes*, 111. As far as I know or can see, this is all Strauss has to say about the complementarity of the two plays.

PART I

On the *Knights*

CHAPTER ONE

Paphlagon: Democracy's Tragic Tendency

The *Knights* begins with a seemingly domestic situation. A slave complains about the abuse he and other slaves have been receiving from their master as a result of a fellow slave, newly bought, evil Paphlagon, and he wishes that the gods would destroy the evil slave (1-5). His wish is joined by a second slave, who curses, in particular, Paphlagon's slanders (6-7). Despite their miserable circumstances, Paphlagon terrifies them so much that neither is willing to even speak of a possible solution (8-20). The second slave suggests that their situation is hopeless when he quotes a line from Euripides, the tragedian, and wonders aloud how he can express their hopelessness "in a smart Euripidean way" (16-18). The first slave, then, reprimands the second slave for his tragic talk, and urges him instead to consider how they may get away from master (19-20).

For a few moments the slaves entertain themselves with the thought of escape, but drop the idea out of fear for their skin lest they get caught (21-29). The second slave then suggests they prostrate themselves before a statue of one of the gods, implying that only divine intervention can save them (30-31). The first slave asks for proof that the gods even exist, implying a disbelief in the gods. As proof, the second slave offers him the example of his own unhappy life, whose misery is so great it cannot be accounted for by earthly causes alone. His proof demonstrates to the first slave that they must look in another direction. If the gods exist but are a source of evils for them they cannot be relied upon for help.

Before considering their next move, the slaves temporarily flee their troubles by stepping outside the play, in order to explain to the audience what is going on:

> We two have a master, violent tempered in a rustic sort of way, a bean-eater, quick to anger—Demos Pnyknitos,[1] a peevish, little old man, somewhat deaf[2] (40-43).

Aristophanes thus makes evident right from the start that our two men are not slaves, but politicians, that the house in which they live is Athens, and that their master is the demos, or the people.

In the *Knights*, there is the greatest divide between the symbols used and the things being symbolized. The symbols are thoroughly private, the things symbolized are thoroughly public: slaves, men with no political status, represent the politicians; a house represents the city; and Demos, the house-master and a private man, represents the people. Why does Aristophanes use private things to represent public things? Does democracy cause political life to be of such a kind that private things yield the best understanding of public things? Why does democracy bring about this result? What consequences does the collapse between the public and the private, implicit here, have for city and man?[3]

Like the symbols of the *Knights*, the plot of the *Knights* collapses the private and the public. On the one hand, the plot has its origin in the private interest of two slaves, on the other, the entire Athenian empire, indeed, the whole Greek world, participates in its outcome. All of the public things that will happen in the play, peace with Sparta, the deposing of Paphlagon, and the people's rejuvenation, derive from the interests and the actions of two slaves striving to escape from their own problems. In portraying a political controversy as if it were a domestic controversy, the beginning of the play and the plot it sets in motion reveal the central theme of the *Knights*. Absolute democracy gives rise to the absolute collapse of the public and the private.

* * * * * * * * * *

The collapse between the public and the private is suggested not only by the symbolism and plot of the play, but by the disposition Aristophanes ascribes to the people in the first sentence of the slave's explanation. For *Demos Pnyknites* is not only a despot in name—that is, he owns slaves—he is a despot in disposition. He regards everything as rightfully his. The people believe they have a right to collapse everything into themselves. The people's belief in this right, or their self-consciousness of their power,[4] gives rise to their angry disposition. *Demos Pnyknites* is always angry because no matter how many beans he eats, or votes he casts, he does not get the satisfaction which as despot he believes he is entitled. Perhaps the people expect to experience the benefits of making the laws, as quickly as one experiences the benefits of eating a bean, so their disappointment and anger are inevitable. Curiously, Aristophanes represents the people as an old man. In Athens the people and the principle of equality rule, but still the people do not seem happy.

Enter Paphlagon:

> Last new moon's day [Demos] bought a slave, tanner[5] Paphlagon, someone most roguish and slandering. He recognized the old man's ways, did leather-Paphlagon, lowered himself before the master, and began fawning, flattering, toadying (43-8).

As the first slave, our narrator, suggests, whereas all of the politicians are slaves to Demos, Paphlagon unlike his colleagues truly embraces the role. He intentionally projects himself as a slave to the people. He responds to the people's apparent inability to find satisfaction by suggesting to them, with his excessive groveling, that as lead politician things will change, because he will fully subordinate himself to them. He acknowledges that he is a lowly servant, making it seem as if he will be the means by which the people achieve absolute self-government. As a true slave, he is a mere extension of them. Ruler and ruled are no longer two, but one. The gap between ruler and ruled has been closed, or so Paphlagon seduces the people to believe.

But as the first slave tells us, the people are wrong, for Paphlagon is guilty of:

> gulling [Demos] with scraps of leather shreds, saying these sorts of things: "Have your bath after trying one case. Put this in your mouth. Eat. Gorge yourself. Have three obols. Do you wish me to feed you a second supper?" (48-52).

Above, our narrator does not tell us the things Paphlagon says to the people, but the "sorts of things" he says.[6] Our narrator, then, invites us to ask the question, what is characteristic about the way Paphlagon speaks to the people?

The first thing we notice is that Paphlagon gives the people one order after another. "Fawning, flattering, toadying" Paphlagon nevertheless speaks to Demos in the imperative. Paphlagon's gestures to the contrary, under his stewardship the people now may be even more the ruled than before. Paphlagon can get away with this, however, because of the kinds of orders he gives. He makes it seem that all of his orders bring the people almost immediate enjoyment. Paphlagon dupes the people into believing that in exchange for their minimal political participation[7] their private needs will be satisfied.

The extent to which Paphlagon's speeches dupe the people can be measured by the extent to which, after first reading them, they dupe us. The first slave's characterization of Paphlagon's words leads us to believe that the people are being bathed and dined right there and then. But this cannot be. The Assembly is not the Prytaneum[8] or the public baths, and Paphlagon is not Praxagora.[9] He is not the communal mother of the people. These are the sorts of things Paphlagon says, not does. But in saying these kinds of things it is as if he did them. For it is his words which he makes into a bath and food for the people. Paphlagon strokes the people with his words. The people find them immediately satisfying. For Paphlagon tells them what they want to hear, as opposed to what they should hear, or what the possible impact of his proposals may be. Therefore his commands are really supplications, and could have been expressed in the interrogative mood, as in his last statement, "Do you wish me to feed you a second supper?", rather than in the imperative. In telling the people what they want to hear, Paphlagon seems like a good slave, and at the same time he seems true to the principle of his regime. For masters do not like to hear displeasing speech from their slaves, and equality dictates that leaders of the people do not know more than the people. If equality is the governing principle, what the people want to hear is the same thing as what they should hear, and their "ruler" makes their desires the authority for their actions.

Telling the people what they want to hear endears Paphlagon to the people, but his words create in the people a craving for something real. His words may be immediately satisfying, but they are not ultimately satisfying. In telling the people what they want to hear, there is enormous pressure on Paphlagon to deliver something. Paphlagon, however, seems too much a creature of his regime to fulfill the people's expectations. That is to say he is too equal, with respect to his ability, to provide for the people, so he must resort to appropriating the services of other politicians.

> And then Paphlagon grabs anything someone of us has prepared, and makes a gift of it to master. Yes, and the other day, when I had kneaded a Laconian barley cake at Pylos, most roguishly he gave me the run around, snatched it up and he himself served it, it having been prepared by me (54-57).

Because Paphlagon endears himself to the people by making it seem that he will satisfy their private needs, all of the politicians are forced to follow suit, even our narrator, whom we now know is Demosthenes—his partner we take to be Nicias.[10] As Demosthenes presents the Spartan hostages to Demos as a meal, as something which provides an immediate private good, he is intercepted by Paphlagon. In order to preserve the illusion that he is the one man who serves their needs, Paphlagon must not only offer them something, he must keep others from doing so. According to Demosthenes, Paphlagon is able to accomplish precisely this:

> For he drives us away, and lets no other minister to master, but standing holding a leather thong while master is dining he scares off the public speakers (58-60).

On the symbolic level, Paphlagon uses a leather thong to stave off the competition. But what happens on the level of reality? What does the leather thong represent?

What makes his rule possible?

Whereas the first half of Demosthenes' explanation of his situation (40-54) is primarily about Paphlagon and Demos, the second half (54-70) is primarily about Paphlagon and the other occupants of the house, i.e. the other politicians. And, as the second half of his explanation shows, Athens is similarly divided. Paphlagon divides the city between himself and Demos on one side, and everyone else on the other.[11] For by engineering lawsuits against his rivals, he keeps them at bay, and protects his own status:

> He chants oracles, and the old man becomes as crazy as the Sibyl.[12] And since Paphlagon sees that master has become entranced, he devises an artful scheme (techne). For those inside he accuses of complete lies; and then we are whipped, while Paphlagon runs around[13] the servants, demanding, harrying, taking bribes, saying this: "Do you see Hylas being whipped on account of me? If you do not change my opinion, you will die today" (61-68).

Successfully chanting oracles, somehow, leads Paphlagon to create a techne, or an art, of leading the people. In other words, Paphlagon has demagoguery down to a science (62-3). This means that Paphlagon has complete control over the people. They are billiard balls on a billiard table, and Paphlagon is Minnesota Fats. The despot has become a slave, and the slave has become a despot. Moreover, *Demos Pnyknites* has become a comic fool. For the people think they are as free as a despot, but in reality they are unequal and unfree. Is this an accidental or necessary result of democracy?

Demosthenes suggests that Demos is most gullible after having heard Paphlagon's oracles. It seems, and the play itself later confirms,[14] that Paphlagon uses his oracles to give expression to the people's prayers, which puts them in a dreamlike state. Paphlagon's oracle chanting is just a more glorified case of his pandering to Demos, of his telling the people what they want to hear. He uses his oracles to persuade the people that the gods sanction the people's prayers, or outlandish hopes, and that he is the one the gods have sent in order to make their prayers a reality. Moreover, Paphlagon's oracle chanting would seem to be necessary in order to justify his own quest for leadership, and the violation of the democratic principle of equality that this quest necessitates. But what is the content of Paphlagon's oracles? For what do the people pray? Given the people's experience of democracy and of equality, what do the people view as the good life?

As we shall later learn, the oracle Demos enjoys hearing the most is the one that foretells that he will "become an eagle amidst the clouds," or, in other words, absolutely free.[15] Absolute freedom is the prayer of the people. Like an eagle the people wish to be free of natural and conventional laws. Like an eagle, they wish to defy gravity, and to eat whenever and to take whatever they want, even the food and possessions belonging to others. Absolute freedom is necessarily the prayer of the people when the principle of equality has been taken to an extreme, as it has in the Athens of the play, where equality has progressed so far that Aristophanes may collapse the individuals comprising the demos into one character. Radical equality leads to the desire for absolute freedom, because radical equality gives rise to the arguments that no one has the superiority to tell another what to do, or how to live, and that all desires and choices are equally worth pursuing, even the desire to become an eagle, or to renounce one's humanity. The people's wish to become an eagle amidst the clouds is not only motivated by the desire to realize absolute freedom, it is not only a wish for the preconditions by which they may live in absolute freedom, it is an expression of the freedom the people already feel. The wish to be an eagle reveals the people's belief that Athenian and Olympian law are mere shackles they can live without. And, Paphlagon's oracle chanting justifies this criminal sensation of freedom. Paphlagon tells the people that they are justified in thinking of themselves as "eagles amidst the clouds," or as absolutely free.

What kind of life, or what kind or regime, will Paphlagon assert comports with the people's wish for and belief in their own freedom? As we shall learn, for Paphlagon, to become absolutely free is to rule the world with an iron fist. Paphlagon is the messiah of imperialism.[16] This is what he means by being an eagle amidst the clouds. Paphlagon is a politician, and a political man to the extreme, as is evident from Demosthenes' depiction of Paphlagon as a slick political operator, and so he supplies the people with a political interpretation of their wish. But is this interpretation really consistent with the people's wish? Or, is it an interpretation that provides him with absolute freedom, while leaving the people free only in their dreams? How will Paphlagon defend his interpretation? Moreover, can one supply another interpretation of absolute freedom more consistent with the people's wish?

Whatever the people's dreams are, Paphlagon's oracle chanting ripens them to hear his indictments. Not only has his oracle chanting made them gullible and favorably disposed towards him, it has put them in a mood to render a verdict. For in response to Paphlagon's oracle chanting, the people cannot help but think of the gods, and of right. And then Paphlagon asks the people to act according to right by rendering a verdict against his rivals. Having endeared himself to the people by catering to their whims and fantasies, having given them cause to believe the gods love them and will fulfill their dreams, Paphlagon is bound to receive the verdict he wants with respect to Demosthenes and the other servants. And so "[they] pay [Paphlagon]; if [they] don't, [they] are stomped on by the old man" (69-70).

No wonder Demosthenes and Nicias were at a loss for something to say, for their situation looks hopeless. The only way for them to save themselves is to reform their regime, but reforming their regime requires they act politically, which is sure to result in their being prosecuted by Paphlagon and punished by the people. Punishment seems almost certain to come, moreover, because in Paphlagon's Athens, the people even experience punishment as their own private good. For the people are paid to hear cases, and those found guilty are forced to pay a public fine.[17] Paphlagon has done to justice the same thing he has done to political rhetoric and to oracles, or religion. He turns it into something which the people experience as immediately gratifying. He makes justice into a private good. Justice has become a private good, both for him and the people.

As leader of the city, Paphlagon embraces a conception of justice that the people find appealing. In Greek, as in English, justice may mean, on the one hand, a high political principle, or right, as in the sentence, "one should do what is right";[18] or, it may mean, paying the penalty, as in the sentence, "I shall get justice from you."[19] Both senses are found in Aristophanes' play, but for Paphlagon, justice is always the latter, because this conception allows him to use even justice as a means to cater to the people, and himself. Filling the city with accusations and indictments, he stimulates the people's appetite for vengeance and then, with a trial, he satisfies it.[20] Moreover, this definition enables him to provide the people with a motive to keep interested in politics. Justice results in a payoff. Unlike Glaucon's and Adeimantus' encounter with Socrates' account of justice, the people experience Paphlagon's definition of justice as an unambiguous good. Under Paphlagon, the people do not wonder about the goodness of justice, or of politics, because politics satisfies a private pleasure. But can political life be sustained on this basis? Is it possible for all political activity to be experienced as merely private pleasure?

After Demosthenes completes his explanation to the audience, he exhorts Nicias to join him in considering "onto which road we ought to turn and to whom" (71-2). Earlier, after reprimanding Nicias for wallowing in tragic talk, Demosthenes urged Nicias to join him in searching for an escape, or a road, from their master (19-20). After his long explanation, it is now apparent to Demosthenes that they need more than a road, they need a man too. Demosthenes' analysis of their situation has apparently taught him that it is not enough for them to discover a road, for neither of them are capable of leading Athens and themselves down it. Athenian democracy has taken such a radical turn towards equality, that neither of them would be found acceptable to the people.

Demosthenes' long explanation has done little for Nicias, however, for all Nicias can do is to repeat his earlier suggestion that they escape (73). Perhaps, in order to force the always cautious Nicias to stand his ground, or perhaps because Paphlagon has indeed already succeeded in expanding his political reach throughout the Greek world, Demosthenes responds by telling Nicias escape is impossible from the ubiquitous Paphlagon (74-79). In light of this, Nicias recommends suicide. Demosthenes, however, cannot go along with this. Demosthenes wants to die manfully (80-1), and suicide, evidently, is not manly. So, Nicias responds with the example of Themistocles. They should kill themselves by drinking bull's blood (82-4).[21] Evidently, Nicias thinks Themistocles' suicide disproves Demosthenes' presumption that all suicide is unmanly. But, what is manly about Themistocles' suicide? By killing himself Themistocles escapes from his promise to help the Persian king defeat Athens. Themistocles killed himself because there was no way to save himself without causing injury to Athens and to his own reputation, as a benefactor of the city. Suicide was therefore a manly course of action for Themistocles, as it is for them, for they have been put in a situation where the only way they can save their lives is by yielding to Paphlagon, thereby contributing to Athens' further corruption. Is democracy also tragically situated? Is there no hope for it too?

Nicias recommends suicide because he thinks they cannot be saved, but his recommendation also seems to suggest that democracy cannot be saved. Why does Nicias recommend suicide, instead of recommending assassination? Why not just kill Paphlagon? The reason seems to be that there are other Paphlagonians,[22] so if they kill Paphlagon, another will just take his place. It seems that it is as inevitable that the people will choose a Paphlagon as it is inevitable that equality generate in the people a wish to be an eagle amidst the clouds. But, what is a Paphlagonian?

From what we have seen so far, Paphlagon is the political man who turns the polis on its head. Under Paphlagon the polis is riven by discord, because Paphlagon uses justice as a sop for the people and a weapon against his enemies. Under Paphlagon the people are led to equate justice with self-interest. Under Paphlagon public speech is impossible, because he creates an atmosphere of terror. Any move against him Paphlagon is able to represent as a move against the people, or as an indictable offense, thereby paralyzing his opposition. It is no accident that Demosthenes must step outside the play in order to explain their circumstances.[23] In the Athens of the play, could the *Knights* be staged? The *Knights* itself represents the city's ability to foster self-understanding, perhaps more so than any other play, for here Aristophanes puts Demos on the stage for all the public to see. In the *Knights*, Aristophanes represents demos in order to enlighten the demos. This play suggests a different political model, that of an upright polis which facilitates public speech and self-awareness, and induces people to reflect upon their polis and themselves. Given the fact that Demosthenes must leave the play in order to tell us what is going on calls to our attention that Paphlagon jeopardizes the city's ability to serve in this regard.

Paphlagon's impact upon the city follows from the fact that he is, as Demosthenes said, an absolute rogue.[24] The word translated "rogue" combines the Greek prefix *pan*, which means all or every, and the word *ergon*, which means work or deed. So, as an absolute rogue, there is nothing Paphlagon would not do, and there is no low to which he would not stoop. In other words, Paphlagon is absolutely free; he is free of moral constraints. Moreover, Paphlagon exploits this freedom to achieve power or absolute freedom over others. For by being a rogue, Paphlagon becomes prime minister of the city, and as such is able to wield the power of imperial Athens. For the people, absolute freedom will always be a dream, a figment of their imaginations. Under Paphlagon, the people are hemmed in by poverty and by one another; imaginary freedom is as close to freedom as they will get. They will have to settle for being equal to the bulk of their fellow citizens. Not so Paphlagon. He leaves behind his former equality, and his life as a lowly tanner,[25] and gains the power and inequality necessary to realize his dream of absolute freedom, which, evidently, his former experience as one of the demos generated in him. Absolute equality generates the wish for absolute freedom, and Paphlagon will make the people sorry that it does. For his experience of absolute freedom comes at their expense.[26]

Whatever a Paphlagonian is, it seems inevitable that the people will chose one as their chief public servant, for if Paphlagon is a representative case, the Paphlagonians embody the principles of the regime.[27] The Paphlagonians are irresistible to the people, because the people see them as reflections of themselves. They come from the gutter, and they do not speak down to the people, at least not while they campaign for office. So what are poor Demosthenes and Nicias to do? Demosthenes' answer: get drunk.

Notes

1. Or, of the Pnyx. The Pnyx is the name of the hill where the Assembly was situated. And, beans were used as a way to cast votes. See Robert Alexander Neil, *The Knights of Aristophanes* (London: Cambridge University Press, 1909), 12, with respect to line 41.

2. Cf. Plato, *Republic*, 488b.

3. Dover sees this "idea" of "presenting Demos as master of a household and politicians as his slaves" as "brilliant" but flawed, because "it is not carried through consistently." As he laments, "purely domestic relationships and purely political relationships run side by side throughout the play, and we have to be prepared for constant shifts from one level to the other." While this seems an accurate description of the way the play proceeds, I differ from Dover in that I do not think this a flaw in the play, but a phenomenon of the drama which cries out for interpretation. The shifting back and forth that Dover notices is significant. It marks the shifting back and forth between the public and the private necessarily occasioned by democracy. One might say that Paphlagon exploits this characteristic of democracy. He makes the public serve the private life of Demos, ultimately to the detriment of Athenian political life, and arguably, Demos' private life as well. Dover, *Aristophanic Comedy* (Berkeley: University of California Press, 1972), 93.

4. Cf. 1111-50.

5. "*Bursodepses*" is a compound noun that could mean skin-softener. This alternative

meaning is interesting in light of the fact that at the end of the play the sausage-seller demonstrates that he is a skin-softener of sorts. He makes old man Demos young and beautiful again (1321ff.), supplying yet another example of his ability to out-Cleon Cleon.

6. Cf. 66.

7. They must judge only one case.

8. In the Prytaneum, Athens provided certain distinguished men with state-provided meals. Cf. 280-3.

9. The democratic heroine of Aristophanes' *Ecclesiazusae*, who turns Athens into a commune.

10. The first slave, our narrator, is Demosthenes, because Demosthenes engineered the Pylos hostage situation to which the slave now refers. The evidence that the second slave is Nicias is perhaps less certain, but seems right in light of this character's religiosity and cautiousness, as well as the fact that Nicias plays a crucial role in the Pylos affair. According to Thucydides' account, it is because Nicias cedes his command to Cleon, that Cleon is able to earn the credit for bringing home the Spartan hostages. See Thucydides, 4.27-28. In any case, the slaves are almost universally understood by scholars to be Demosthenes and Nicias. However, De Ste. Croix and Dover do not think the second slave is Nicias. See G.E.M. De Ste. Croix, "The Political Outlook of Aristophanes" in Segal, 51 and note 14.

11. Cf. 813-19.

12. Sybil was a renowned prophetess.

13. "Runs around," in Greek *peritheon*. It combines the prefix, *peri*, which may mean, around or beyond, and the verb, *theo*, which means, to run. If you separate the prefix and the verb, and treat *theon* as the genitive plural of *theos*, "god," we could for a moment hear, "while Paphlagon beyond the gods was . . . ."

14. See 809, 997-1099, especially 1011-13 and 1086-87.

15. 1011-3. Compare this and 1086-7 with 792-809.

16. 792-800.

17. See 255-7, 1358-61.

18. See 258, and context.

19. See 347, and context.

20. 235-39, 255-7, 278-9, 284, 300-12, 429-46, 475-9, et al.

21. The actual cause of Themistocles' death is a matter of dispute. Thucydides alludes to the opinion that he committed suicide by drinking poison, although he seems to side with the view that he died from an illness. Thucydides, 1.138.4. Plutarch refers to the "usual story" of his suicide by bull's blood. Plutarch: *The Lives of the Noble Grecians and Romans*, trans. John Dryden (New York: Modern Library, 1992): 154.

22. 6.

23. Demosthenes steps out of the play in that at 35-36 he explicitly recognizes the spectators, and in 40-70 becomes Aristophanes' narrator. It must be stated that Aristophanes frequently breaks the dramatic illusion. Furthermore, *Wasps*, *Peace* and *Birds* feature a break of the dramatic illusion similar to that of the *Knights*. One of the participating characters tells us the situation that the characters are in. See Dover, *Aristophanic Comedy*, 54 passim.

24. *Panourgataton*, 45; cf. 249-50, 317, 331. Aristophanes puts this adjective in the superlative. Literally, it might mean, "rogue-est" or "biggest rogue."

25. See Neil, *The Knights*, 13, 44.

26. 792-6, 813-9.

27. See Croiset, *Aristophanes*, 82-3 for a different opinion. According to Croiset, the Cleon of the play "is emphatically not a human being, and for this reason cannot really be the personification of a class of real men" (83). According to Croiset, "hatred and violent prejudice" so "obscure his [Aristophanes'] vision" that his rendering of the real Cleon is nothing more than a vicious and unrepresentative parody.

CHAPTER TWO

Demosthenes' Comic Plan

Nicias' suggestion that they drink bull's blood, i.e., commit suicide, gives Demosthenes another idea. Rather than drink bull's blood, Demosthenes recommends they drink "pure wine from the good god."

> For perhaps then we might figure out something useful (85-86).

Nicias, however, objects. He doubts that "becoming drunk" would have this effect (87-88), just as Demosthenes earlier doubted the existence of the gods.[1] And, just as Demosthenes' doubt forces Nicias to present his proof of the gods' existence, Nicias' doubt forces Demosthenes to present his proof of wine's usefulness:

> Do you see? Whenever human beings drink, then they're rich, they're successful, they win their lawsuits, they're happy, they help their friends. Here, fetch me a jug of wine, in order that I may irrigate my mind and say something ingenious (91-96).

Although wine is capable of having an inspirational effect, Demosthenes' proof of wine's usefulness is as ridiculous as Nicias' proof of the existence of the gods. Nicias derived the gods' existence from the fact that his life is miserable. His miserable life proved the gods hate him, which proved the gods exist, but might not his miserable life be due to chance, or to himself? In Demosthenes' proof, from the fact that human beings drink and have assorted good things happen to them, Demosthenes asserts that wine is the cause of these good things, but correlation does not prove causation. In Nicias' view, because of the gods, he is bound to fail. Not surprisingly, he finally recommends suicide. In Demosthenes' view, because of wine, he is bound to succeed. Not surprisingly, he contrives a plan that induces him to place his, Nicias' and Athens' fate in the hands of the first sausage-seller who happens by. Taken to an extreme, both wine-drinking and democracy make it impossible for human beings to draw distinctions, for both lead one to see all things as equal. Therefore, both lead human beings to make decisions based upon the lot. It is fitting that Demosthenes' plan begins with wine. For it begins with that which blinds human beings to distinctions, and ends with a political regime which annihilates distinctions within the city.

Although Demosthenes' speech on wine does not fully convince Nicias (97), he obeys Demosthenes and fetches some wine from within master's house (101). Whether master's wine will help Demosthenes "scatter this whole place with little plans, thoughts, and ideas" is unknown (99-100), but the mere talk of wine has a desirable effect on Nicias. Whereas before he was too afraid to even say what they should do (17), now he boldly goes into the house, and returns with the wine. Demosthenes takes the opportunity to ask Nicias what Paphlagon is doing, and is told that "the slanderous one snores drunk on his hides" (103-4).[2] Then, Demosthenes takes a drink of wine, and immediately afterward, or so it seems, hits upon a plan, for he proclaims:

> Oh good god, the plan is yours, not mine (108).

Upon hearing this, Nicias is anxious for Demosthenes to share his "god's plan" with him, but to his chagrin learns that Demosthenes' plan is for him to go quickly into the house again in order to steal Paphlagon's oracles, "while he sleeps" (109-10). Although Nicias fears that Demosthenes' god may be evil rather than good (111-2), he immediately goes back into the house. Meanwhile, Demosthenes, again, grabs the wine and repeats his earlier proclamation, that he shall drink "in order that I may irrigate my mind and say something ingenious"[3] (114). But has not Demosthenes already said something ingenious, at least to himself, for he just thanked god for bestowing upon him a plan? Does he have his plan or not?

No sooner does Demosthenes finish his cup of wine than Nicias comes back. He reports that Paphlagon is still sleeping, and therefore "missed me taking his sacred oracle, the very one he was guarding most" (115-7). Now, how Nicias can say that Paphlagon is guarding anything, closely or not, at the very moment he is drunk and asleep, or why Nicias did not notice Paphlagon and "his sacred oracle" on his first trip, apparently having noticed the smell of alcohol on Paphlagon's breath, is a mystery. Did Nicias really take Paphlagon's most prized oracle, or does he just say this to please Demosthenes? Perhaps he lost his nerve and took the first oracle he could get his hands on. Whatever the case may be, Demosthenes is overjoyed. He calls Nicias "wisest man," requests the oracle and a cup of wine, and then proceeds to read and drink, ignoring Nicias' demand to know what the oracle says as well as his comic remarks (119-124). Finally, after apparently having read and interpreted the oracle, Demosthenes has his answer: the oracle Nicias stole, Paphlagon was guarding closely for "a long time," because "herein is contained how the man himself is to die" (125-127).

Understandably, Nicias wants to know how the oracle shows this (128). But, rather than tell Nicias what the oracle says about the future, which is what Nicias wants to know, Demosthenes tells him what it says about the past, or what Nicias already knows. Then, despite the fact that according to Demosthenes "the oracle speaks clearly," Demosthenes proceeds to paraphrase it. If the oracle is so clear, which is strange in itself since oracles are notoriously unclear, why not just read it?[4] What is going on here?

Demosthenes tells Nicias what the oracle says about the past in order to get Nicias to accept what the oracle says about the future, that they and Athens are to be saved by a sausage-seller. According to Demosthenes, the oracle says "how first a hemp-seller comes to be, who will first control the affairs of the city." And that afterward "a sheep-seller is second," who rules "until another more disgusting man than he should arise, and after that he dies." For "leather-seller Paphlagon succeeds him"[5] (128-137).

Demosthenes uses the oracle to show Nicias that the history of democracy is one of decline. The hemp-seller and the sheep-seller refer to previous Athenian politicians. In the beginning there is a hemp-seller, who is succeeded by a disgusting sheep-seller,[6] who is himself destroyed by Paphlagon who is even more disgusting. Furthermore, whereas the transition from the first to the second demagogue just seems to happen, it is suggested that the third, Paphlagon, comes to power because he topples the second. Succession requires destruction. As the men at the top become more disgusting they use their power to undo one another. Political life begins to look barbaric.

But not only does Demosthenes' interpretation of the oracle suggest that democracy necessitates decline, it also suggests that the private dominates the public. All of Athens' rulers are said to be salesmen. The *polis* (city) is dominated by the *polai* (salesmen). And the salesman (*poles*) replaces the orator (*rhetor*). This comes out even clearer in the Greek, as here Aristophanes has both characters use the Greek word, *poles*, or seller, by itself, separated from the product being sold. In Greek, one is a "*poles*" of something, i.e., a hempseller or a sheepseller, not simply a *poles*.[7] But, Nicias, after learning that Paphlagon was predestined to rule Athens, exclaims:

> Oh misery. If only from somewhere there would arise one more seller (*poles*) (139-40).

Since democracy means the rule of the people, and the people view happiness in terms of the private, salesmen come to be the best politicians, because they are habituated to cater to private desires. And the most unbeatable politician of all would be the one who is pure salesman, someone capable of selling any product or of convincing the people he can satisfy whatever desire the people might have.

Demosthenes' interpretation of the oracle so well prepares Nicias for the oracles' final revelation that shocked as he is to hear it, he submits to its prescription:

> D: The man who will expel Paphlagon is a sausage-seller.
> N: A sausage-seller? Oh Poseidon, what a profession. Let's see, where shall we find this man? (143-5).

Given the historical account that Demosthenes provides Nicias, that a sausage-seller should be the one who expels Paphlagon, makes sense. Mashing animal stomachs into sausage seems even more disgusting than working on the skins of animals, so the oracle's prediction continues the existing trend. And he is a salesman, practiced at catering to a basic human desire, the desire for food. The products associated with each salesman suggest that the city is moving more and more towards the private. Paphlagon is a tanner, whose products are used for clothing—a visible covering which masks the private. The sausage-seller's products are mashed up stomachs produced for the stomach—an invisible, or private organ. But while this explains how Demosthenes gets an aristocrat to support a man even more base than Paphlagon, why will Demosthenes himself support this man? Is he, like Nicias, persuaded by the oracle? Has the man who a moment ago doubted the gods' existence suddenly found religion? Has the man who a moment ago stated that Paphlagon made Demos "crazy as the Sybil" with an oracle himself been made crazy with an oracle?[8] And, if Demosthenes does not really believe the oracle, why would he accept as his savior the first sausage-seller who happens by?

In response to Nicias' question about where the sausage-seller will be found, Demosthenes says, "Let us look for him" (146).[9] Miraculously, in the very next moment Nicias spots one:

> But here one comes, as if by the grace of god, going to market (146-7).

Demosthenes then summons the sausage-seller over in dramatic language, addressing him as "savior to the city and to us."[10] As one would expect, the sausage-seller is incredulous. Demosthenes continues on in the same way, beseeching the sausage-seller to come towards them, "so that you may learn how lucky you are and how greatly blessed" (150-1). Nicias tells Demosthenes to get to the point, "explain to him the meaning of the god's oracle." Demosthenes, however, speaks another twenty lines before he even mentions the oracle and forty before he reads it. Religiously devoted Nicias is ready to put everything in the hands of the gods, just as previously he recommended they prostrate themselves before a statue of one of the gods. So caught up is he in the apparent miracle of the sausage-seller's appearance that he forgets that the oracle he and Demosthenes have been following is said to be of Bacis not Apollo. It is not the "god's oracle," but an oracle from a deceased soothsayer.[11]

In delaying his presentation of the oracle to the sausage-seller, Demosthenes seems to recognize that the sausage-seller is probably not like Nicias. That is to say, Demosthenes cannot count on the sausage-seller's religiosity. Rather, he has to give him arguments. The arguments he gives help us understand why Demosthenes is willing to go along with the oracle's prescription, and at the same time, present us with his understanding of democracy.

That the sausage-seller needs convincing the sausage-seller himself makes evident. After Demosthenes again tries to entice the sausage-seller into becoming his protege by heaping compliments upon him (157-9), the sausage-seller responds, quite reasonably:

> Oh good fellow, why won't you let me wash my tripe and sell my sausages, instead of mocking me? (160-1).

The sausage-seller is a private man who wants to tend to his own affairs, and who believes that as a common man this is his lot in life. Whereas in speaking with Nicias, Demosthenes had to address the problem of how one gets an aristocrat to support a base man, in speaking with the sausage-seller, Demosthenes must address two problems: how to make a private man, an *idiotes*, interested in political matters? And, how to convince him he is worthy of rule?

Even before the sausage-seller asks to be left alone, Demosthenes has already begun answering the first question, how to interest a private man in political matters. For in alluding to the sausage-seller's future as head slave, he addresses him as commander (*tage*), or someone with absolute authority.[12] And, as Demosthenes suggests, with absolute authority, the sausage-seller will be able to satisfy any desire no matter what it is:

> Over all these [pointing to the audience] you yourself shall be the paramount chief,[13] and of the market,[14] the harbors and the Pnyx. You'll trample the Senate, humble the generals, you'll chain, you'll imprison, you'll brothelize the Prytaneum (166-7).

Demosthenes makes it seem that the sausage-seller's power in Athens will be unlimited. He will control domestic and international affairs as well as the making of policy.

Furthermore, as absolute ruler, the sausage-seller will be able to punish office holders, or anyone who enjoys an elevated position. Demosthenes seems to be evoking the resentment he expects the sausage-seller to have, as a representative of the lowest class, towards those in power, men of distinction. But as Demosthenes suggests, the sausage-seller will be able to do much more than vent his class envy. As absolute ruler, anything goes. Political power will enable the sausage-seller to make low the high, and to make the high serve the low. The sausage-seller will be able to convert the Prytaneum into a brothel. In the Prytaneum, Athens honors its most distinguished citizens with state-provided meals. By turning the Prytaneum into a brothel, the sausage-seller will be able to assert his supremacy over those previously above him and at the same time experience sexual pleasure. It is no accident that Demosthenes mentions sex. The way to make politics appealing to a private man is to show that politics will enable him to enjoy life's greatest private pleasure anytime he wishes. And, Demosthenes makes evident that he can exploit Athens' imperial possessions with the same freedom. As Demosthenes promises, from "Caria" to "Carthage," "all this is to be sold at your will"(168-76). In other words, politics offers the sausage-seller not only the greatest private pleasure, but also the greatest variety of pleasures.

Demosthenes attempts to get the sausage-seller to enter politics without mentioning anything political, or public. To the extent Demosthenes raises the issue of the public realm it is only to point out that as leader the sausage-seller will be able to collapse everything public into himself. Everything outside him will be an extension of him. Although Demosthenes is exaggerating in order to interest the sausage-seller in politics, the rule of the sausage-seller, as we shall see, will turn Demosthenes' exaggeration into a reality. Under the sausage-seller, the public realm disappears to an even greater extent than Demosthenes' exaggeration depicts.

One might say that according to Demosthenes' depiction, the sausage-seller will be a tyrant in the fashion of a Hiero,[15] or a Persian king. He will be in charge of the public realm, and as a result will be able to satisfy any private desire. Demosthenes supposes that the public realm survives intact despite its seeming disappearance in a sea of private pleasure. The sausage-seller will rule "the market, harbors and Pnyx." The existing distinction between these realms is maintained. In the market, Athenians tend to their own affairs; in the Pnyx, public policy is decided. To maintain a distinction between these two places is to maintain a distinction between what goes on in both. Demosthenes fails to see that in defending the political with reference to the private he fails to provide a basis for maintaining this distinction.

Demosthenes also assumes a distinction between international and domestic commerce when he distinguishes the agora from the harbors, ignoring the fact that maintaining this distinction requires the recognition of the political. Presumably, the regulation befitting the harbors differs from the regulation befitting the agora, inasmuch as international trade differs from domestic trade. With international trade, the question of national interest is more likely to come into play. For example, with respect to international trade, cities sometimes impose trade embargoes on one another. Eliminate the public as a reason for acting and you eliminate the distinction between domestic and international trade, just as surely as you eliminate the distinction between Athens and other cities.[16]

Having presented the sausage-seller with this alluring image, Demosthenes supposes that he has been sold on the goodness of politics. So now he attempts to bring in the oracle, presumably, in order to convince the sausage-seller that not only is politics desirable, but that he is meant for it.

> For as this here oracle says, you are to become a great man (177-8).

To Demosthenes' regret, however, the sausage-seller has no interest in hearing the oracle:

> Tell me, and how am I—a sausage-seller—going to become a man?[17] (178-9).

The sausage-seller finds doubtful that he can become even a man, let alone a great man, and apparently nothing that Demosthenes' oracle has to say is capable of convincing him otherwise. So, without reference to the oracle, Demosthenes next tries to convince the sausage-seller that he is qualified:[18]

> It's on account of exactly that, don't you see, that you are to become great, because you're base, from the market, and bold[19] (180-1).

Although the sausage-seller's baseness and his being from the market are self-evident, his boldness is not. How can Demosthenes say the sausage-seller is bold when the sausage-seller has just said, unboldly, that being a sausage-seller he cannot believe that he might become a man? He seems to lack the very quality one needs in order to accept the call to greatness, the belief in one's greatness.

That Demosthenes ascribes a characteristic to the sausage-seller which is the exact opposite to the one the sausage-seller himself demonstrates reveals that Demosthenes realizes that his selection of the sausage-seller is arbitrary. For Demosthenes abstracts from the particular characteristics of this man. According to Demosthenes, any man will do, because Athenian democracy has regressed to the point that the basest and most common man is bound to win Demos' approval. Demosthenes thinks Athens has hit bottom. The sausage-seller will prove it still has further to fall. The full implications of the arguments Demosthenes is about to make, the sausage-seller will later make manifest.

The sausage-seller is not persuaded by Demosthenes' explanation, and says that he "does not deem himself worthy to hold great power" (182). The sausage-seller, the representative democratic figure, here expresses an aristocratic principle: people should do only what they are worthy of. As expected, this distresses Demosthenes, for as long as the sausage-seller maintains this principle, he cannot be persuaded to go along with Demosthenes' plan. So Demosthenes cleverly responds,

> Oh misery, whatever's the matter that you should say that you yourself are not worthy? You seem to be conscious of something beautiful in yourself. You're not of the beautiful and good? (183-5).

The "something beautiful" to which Demosthenes refers, and which the sausage-seller is supposedly conscious of is difficult to know. Could it be justice? For the sausage-seller's sentiment that one should do only what one is worthy of doing looks something like the definition of justice in the *Republic*. Every man has one expertise and therefore one job.[20] Or is it moderation? For the sausage-seller in holding back shows both self-restraint and self-knowledge. Whatever the case may be, Demosthenes' suggestion that the sausage-seller is beautiful, as he stands there holding the guts of animals, seems ironic to say the least. His question leaves no doubt about it. He well knows that the sausage-seller is not of the beautiful and good. He is no gentleman. The purpose of Demosthenes' remark is to remind the sausage-seller that as a non-gentleman, as a low man, he is not expected to exercise virtue, or to forego an opportunity merely because he is not worthy of it. He should do whatever the occasion affords. For this is how low men behave. Demosthenes uses the sausage-seller's principle to overcome the sausage-seller's principle. For he suggests that as a low man the sausage-seller is not worthy of noble thoughts, and therefore should leap at the opportunity that the gods, or at least Demosthenes, offers him. If one should do only what one is worthy of, then the sausage-seller has no business holding noble thoughts.

When the sausage-seller responds as Demosthenes expects swearing to the gods that his roots are entirely "base," this gives Demosthenes the opportunity to tell the sausage-seller "what a good thing" this is for "political life" (186-7). It is a good thing to be base, Demosthenes would have the sausage-seller think, because the base do not let principle stand in the way of their own happiness. Demosthenes seems to think that the sausage-seller will be able to conquer Paphlagon with nothing but unrestrained viciousness.

Still, the sausage-seller persists in his self-doubt:

> But, good fellow, I have no knowledge of the liberal arts, except letters, and I'm proper bad at that (188-9).

The sausage-seller's stubborn refusal to yield forces Demosthenes to make plain the advantages of baseness:

> This only hurts you, that you know them at all, even proper bad. For demagoguery is no longer for a man of the liberal arts, or of good qualities, but for one ignorant and foul (190-3).

Democracy means no distinctions. Whatever sets human beings apart, whether it is virtue, beauty, education, or even leadership ability, disqualifies one from being leader. The sausage-seller's stubbornness forces Demosthenes to make a radically egalitarian argument, so that the sausage-seller will deem himself worthy to rule. Democracy is the rule of the equal. According to democracy's principle, that the sausage-seller is completely lacking in distinction not only does not disqualify him, it proves he is right for the job.

Demosthenes' arguments in defense of equality are as ridiculous as his previous argument in defense of politics. The sausage-seller is worthy because there is nothing worthy about him. While this argument may prove that the sausage-seller satisfies the radical egalitarian principle that Demosthenes suggests now reigns in Athens, it says nothing about how someone without "good qualities" can do battle with and defeat the most powerful man in Athens. Although the rest of the play vindicates Demosthenes' faith in the sausage-seller, since the sausage-seller defeats Paphlagon, Demosthenes' arguments go unvindicated. The sausage-seller succeeds not because he is base or common, but because he proves to be a man of extraordinary ingenuity.[21] Moreover, whereas Demosthenes believes he understands the implications of democracy, i.e., radical egalitarianism, about this too, the sausage-seller will show, Demosthenes requires education. Demosthenes assumes radical egalitarianism is the final stage of democracy, and because Athens has reached that stage, any man will do. The rest of the play proves Demosthenes wrong on both counts. Any man will not do, and radical egalitarianism is not the final stage of democracy.

After Demosthenes makes the point that demagoguery is now for the "uneducated and the foul," again he attempts to introduce the oracle (193-4). The sausage-seller now complies, asking Demosthenes "what the oracle says" (195). In presenting the oracle (195-201), Demosthenes attempts to generate awe in the sausage-seller. First, he introduces it as "wrapped in rather complex and riddling language,"[22] and then he recites it in the oracular style,[23] rather than paraphrasing it as he did with Nicias. Since Nicias is a believer, all he needs is the meaning. Since the sausage-seller is at least skeptical, Demosthenes supposes he needs special effects.

Despite being presented with the oracle, and being shown that the oracle predicts that a sausage-seller will overthrow Paphlagon, the sausage-seller remains doubtful:[24]

> The oracle flatters me. But I wonder how I am supposed to be able to govern the people (211-2).

Aikallo, the word translated here as "flatter," appears at 48, where Demosthenes describes the way Paphlagon wins the approval of Demos. In having the sausage-seller use the same word as Demosthenes uses to describe Paphlagon, Aristophanes suggests to us that Demosthenes treats the sausage-seller in the same way that Paphlagon treats Demos: he begins by offering the sausage-seller material comforts, and then he tries to make him crazy with an oracle. That the sausage-seller does not respond as Demos would suggests, unbeknownst to Demosthenes, that though he may be of the Demos, the sausage-seller is not demos-like.

Demosthenes has an ingenious solution to the sausage-seller's self-doubt:

> Easiest deed. Do the same things you do already. Mix up and mash all the political affairs together, and always win over Demos by enticing him with little rhetorical dishes (213-6).

Like Demosthenes' previous arguments, this one supplies an exaggeration tailor-made to persuade the sausage-seller. Demosthenes combats the sausage-seller's doubts about whether he knows how to rule the people by telling the sausage-seller that he already knows, for the demagogic art and the sausage-selling art involve the same activity. Both demagoguery and sausage-selling combine parts indiscriminately to form a whole, the character of which is so confused all the original parts can no longer be recognized. Both form a chaotic whole. And, both make these chaotic wholes appealing or appetizing, and profit from them. Of course, the fact that both involve mixing does not mean that to know how to do the one is to know how to do the other.[25] Sausage-selling is a metaphor for demagoguery, it is not equal to it. And, as a metaphor, it simplifies. But as with Demosthenes' previous arguments this one gives us a picture of what democracy looks like when taken to an extreme.

According to Demosthenes' earlier account (40-70), the demagogue slavishly caters to the desires of Demos. So nothing exists to regulate these desires. Although the demagogue is able to manipulate Demos, he will not provide order to Demos' desires, since he benefits from the resulting disorder. In an atmosphere of chaos, the demagogue has an easier time gulling Demos into doing what he wants.[26] Moreover, providing order means telling Demos "no," which demagogues are reluctant to do. But whether or not there is a demagogue at the top of a radical democracy does not seem to matter, for the principle of equality generates the same result. According to the principle of equality all desires are equal, and deserve equal consideration. Democracy calls for pluralism. But without an undemocratic principle to organize or provide a hierarchy to Demos' desires, political affairs are bound to become unintelligible, like the inside of a sausage. If this is true, it would seem that democracy introduces arbitrariness into the city. For if there is no way to understand what is going on, there is no way to diagnose whether laws are having the desired effect. Politics is no longer an expression of human agency, because it is no longer possible to link cause and effect. Ironically, if one makes a law out of every desire, whether any desire gets satisfied is purely a matter of chance.

In order to persuade the sausage-seller to challenge Paphlagon and become the new leader of the people, Demosthenes provides him with a picture of democracy he hopes the sausage-seller will not be able to resist. He presents an extreme exaggeration of democracy designed to persuade a man he expects embodies democracy's underlying principles—freedom and equality. For Demosthenes tells him that as demagogue he will have absolute freedom, and that absolute equality now reigns in Athens. Demosthenes tells the sausage-seller that Athenian political life is such as to make him feel thoroughly at home in politics. Being demagogue will bring him absolute happiness, for he can satisfy any desire, and he will never feel inadequate because equality has become perfectly manifest in the city. In providing this caricature of democracy, Demosthenes presupposes that he knows what democracy looks like at the extreme, or that he knows what kind of a city the perfectly democratic man would be at home in. The sausage-seller will show him that he does not, for by the end of the play he makes known his own democratic exaggeration: a rejuvenated Demos who leaves behind the Pnyx and political life, and returns to the countryside where he can enjoy a lifetime of sexual pleasure (1316-1408). The political is totally eliminated from the life of Demos. And, Demosthenes, the man who only a little while ago discovered the sausage-seller, is silent. Thus, it is the end of logos and rhetoric, as well as politics—and if the end of logos then the end of poetry.

Demosthenes' plan is comic, in the beginning, because it supposes that a man chosen at random can defeat omnipotent and ruthless Paphlagon. And, in the end, because it works for reasons that have little to do with those he cites. The sausage-seller is victorious not because he is ordinary, but because he is extraordinary. And it is because he is extraordinary that he ends up teaching Demosthenes what he thought he knew—the meaning of absolute democracy. Demosthenes is once again outwitted by a man from the market.[27] Perhaps it is for this reason that the poet does not dignify Demosthenes' character with a name. By the end of the play it is Demosthenes, not the sausage-seller, who remains anonymous.[28]

Notes

1. 30-34.

2. So much for the power of wine.

3. Cf. 96.

4. See 195-201. As Aristophanes allows us to see for ourselves, and as Demosthenes admits, the oracle is not so clear.

5. Sommerstein, citing J. Kirchner, *Prosopographia Attica* (Berlin 1901-3), 5759, states that the hemp-seller is Eucrates, and that "nothing is known of his political career." Alan Sommerstein, *Aristophanes: Knights* (Wilts: Aris & Phillips, Ltd., 1981): 150. The sheep-seller is Lysicles, who is called such by Plutarch in his account of Pericles. Citing Aeschines, Plutarch states that Lysicles came to be chief man in Athens by taking Aspasia (Pericles' mistress) into his company after Pericles' death. Plutarch, 200. Lysicles himself died in 428. Thucydides, 3.19.2. However, "[o]ne should not attach too much importance to the 'succession of the three merchants,' which has been so meekly accepted on the testimony of Aristophanes (*Knights*, 129)." Croiset, *Aristophanes*, 1909. Dover states that according to ancient commentators the sheep-seller may be Kallias or Lysicles, but adds "there is no historical evidence for the political domination of Athens of any of these men between the death of Pericles and the rise of Cleon." Dover, *Aristophanic Comedy*, 93.

6. This is suggested by the fact that Paphlagon is said to be more disgusting.

7. See Neil, *The Knights of Aristophanes*, 24, and Sommerstein, *Knights*, 150, with respect to line 131.

8. 61-63.

9. If Demosthenes were a true believer there would be no need for them to look.

10. The oracle nowhere says that the sausage-seller is a savior, or that this sausage-seller is *the* sausage-seller. Again, Demosthenes is interpreting.

11. See 123,124.

12. Cf. Neil. *Tagos* is "a favorite Aeschylean word to express the haughty ruler." Neil, *Knights*, 29, with respect to line 159.

13. *Archelas* (paramount chief) appears at *Persians*, 297, in the mouth of the queen of Persia, King Darius' wife, in reference to the Persian captains. Taken literally, *Archelas* might be translated, "people-leader," although as far as I know no one translates it this way. It combines the words *arche*, leader, and *laos*, common people, or the subjects of a prince. Although this alternative translation is not used, I point it out because it illustrates one of the difficulties Aristophanes presents us in the *Knights*. He forces us to recognize two peoples: on the one hand, Demos, and on the other, the many and various individuals of Athens. Cf. 223-4, 227, 260-5, et al. So, Demos is and is not the people. One may get at the same point through observing that above Demosthenes points to the audience while using a plural demonstrative adjective. Thus, he is speaking to the demos about Demos, as of course Aristophanes is doing.

14. "Market" translates "agora," a public place where people converse and trade. Cf. 1373-80.

15. Xenophon's *Hiero* provides a similar account of the benefits of rule.

16. By the end of the play, Demos has become the "monarch" of Greece. (1329-30, 1333-4). And Paphlagon is taken to the gates of the city where the foreigners whom he used

to harass can see him (1407-8). Paphlagon becomes a symbol of Athens' new openness to strangers. Cf. Thucydides, 2.38 and 39.

17. In Greek, an *aner*, or a real man. Or as Strauss puts it, an "hombre." *Socrates and Aristophanes*, 83.

18. Nicias thought all that had to be done was for Demosthenes to give the sausage-seller the oracle. As it will turn out, the oracle is not enough. Demosthenes must supply a rational argument.

19. *Thrasus* can simply mean bold, but is most frequently used in a pejorative sense to describe the quality of taking action in a reckless way.

20. Except, of course, the philosopher-king.

21. 1319-23, 1335-8.

22. See above, with respect to 128, and note. Although at 204, in response to a question, Demosthenes says "it [the oracle] speaks for itself." At 206, again in response to a question, he says, "this [the oracle's meaning] is most plain."

23. See Neil, *Knights*, 33 with respect to 197, and Sommerstein, *Knights*, with respect to 197-201.

24. Does the sausage-seller see what we see, that neither the oracle nor Demosthenes' interpretation of the oracle says that this sausage-seller is *the* sausage-seller? Perhaps one could argue that the oracle does persuade the sausage-seller. It persuades him that he will become demagogue, and now he wants to know how to be demagogue. However, at 222, the sausage-seller asks, "Who will be my ally?" Evidently, he remains doubtful even about whether he will become demagogue.

25. Cf. 1395-9.

26. 864-7.

27. Cleon outwits Demosthenes at Pylos. See Thucydides' account, 4. 1-41, or lines 54-6.

28. See chapter 1. Not once during the play does the name "Demosthenes" appear. Whereas at 1257, the sausage-seller is revealed to be Agoracritus. Nicias' name also never appears, however Aristophanes makes clear that Nicias is much less important than Demosthenes. He is an errand boy for Demosthenes, and is not heard from again after the entrance of the sausage-seller.

CHAPTER THREE

The Deposing of Zeus

As soon as Demosthenes finishes preparing the sausage-seller, or so it seems, Paphlagon emerges from the house making accusations. Paphlagon's stormy entrance so intimidates the sausage-seller that he starts to run away. Right at this moment Demosthenes summons the knights, and the sausage-seller holds his ground (235-46). For approximately the next 200 lines, Paphlagon attempts to frighten the sausage-seller into withdrawing, but is unsuccessful. So Paphlagon takes his case to the Senate,[1] with the sausage-seller right behind him. While Paphlagon and the sausage-seller square off in the Senate, Aristophanes has the knights present the parabasis.[2] And, just as the parabasis reveals the character of Aristophanes, the Senate scene—of which we will get an account immediately after the parabasis—reveals the character of the sausage-seller. During the parabasis, Aristophanes loses his anonymity. He tells the public who he is and what he stands for. During the Senate contest we learn what the sausage-seller stands for. We learn what his principles are and the implications his principles have for political life.

It may be the case that Aristophanes inserts a Senate debate into the play for the purpose of revealing to us the meaning of the sausage-seller. For, as we shall see, the Senate contest has no impact upon the plot of the play. At the conclusion of the Senate contest, the Senate rules that the "war continues" (673). At the conclusion of the play, Demos accepts Sparta's peace terms (1388-93). Regardless of the Senate's ruling, the war is over. The Senate might as well never have convened, for Demos does not even acknowledge its existence. Furthermore, the Senate debate has no bearing on the battle being waged between Paphlagon and the sausage-seller, because it is the contest before Demos that will determine the winner.[3] The Senate is powerless to affect the policy of Athens as it pertains to the outside world—i.e., the war, or the inside world—i.e., Athens' leadership. So, one might say this scene serves to show not only the significance of the sausage-seller, but the irrelevance of the Senate, and is thus another sign of Athens' degenerate state.

Other than Paphlagon acknowledging he lost the Senate contest (722-3), everything we learn about the contest in the Senate comes from the sausage-seller's narration. Neither we, who listen to the parabasis while it occurs, nor the knights, who deliver the parabasis, see it. Can the sausage-seller's narration be trusted given the fact that, as will soon be clear, he is even more a rogue than Paphlagon, and given the fact that by distorting the facts he may gain the knights' affection? The sausage-seller's narration may tell us what he wished had happened rather than what actually happened. But it is what he wished had happened that is important, perhaps more so than what "actually" happened, if through the sausage-seller's narration Aristophanes attempts to reveal what he represents. If we are trying to understand the sausage-seller, or what he represents, there is no better place to look than his own vision of what it means to score a political victory, whether this victory occurs in the way he says or not.

The parabasis ends the moment the sausage-seller returns from his contest in the Senate. Upon seeing the sausage-seller, the knights say that his absence worried them (612). They are anxious to know how he fared. After the sausage-seller tells them he has become Nikeboule, or Senate Victor, the knights are very pleased (616-7). They beseech the sausage-seller to tell them everything clearly, boasting that "[they] would be willing to take a long journey in order to hear it" (621-2). In the sentence preceding the one quoted, the chorus leader praises the sausage-seller for both his speeches and what he has accomplished—his deeds (618-20). The chorus, while recognizing that both the sausage-seller's speeches and deeds are praiseworthy, because both work towards the overthrow of Paphlagon, seems unaware of the inconsistency between its own speeches and deeds. They say they would travel a long distance to hear the sausage-seller's account of his Senate victory, but they were unwilling to travel a short distance to hear it firsthand, to say nothing about helping him win it. Their speeches convey concern, their deeds apathy.

In order to induce the sausage-seller to tell them everything, the knights address the sausage-seller as "best one" and tell him "to take courage and speak, as we are all pleased with you" (622-4). The knights' encouragement evidently works, for the sausage-seller proceeds to give his longest speech of the play in which he includes every sordid detail (624-82). Why would the knights beckon to hear all, when they did not think it worth their while to see anything? Earlier in the play (222-6) in response to the sausage-seller's question to Demosthenes regarding who his allies will be, Demosthenes tells him that his allies will be, among others, the knights. If the Senate confrontation was so important that the knights require a clear and complete account of it, and if it was so important that the knights were worried during the sausage-seller's absence, why do they cease to be his allies in the Senate and make him fight alone? On the other hand, if the battle was unimportant—as the plot of the *Knights* suggests—and it was for this reason that they stayed behind, why do they require the sausage-seller's complete account?

When the sausage-seller left for the Senate, he was nameless. He is no longer even properly regarded a sausage-seller, as Aristophanes suggests, when he has the sausage-seller tell us before he leaves that he drops his stomachs and knives (488-9). In that he is indistinguishable from any one else, one might say that he is any man. He thus embodies the democratic principle of equality, for according to this principle, any man will do. Taken to its extreme this principle means that all men are the same, or cannot be distinguished from one another. In the time it takes the knights to deliver the parabasis, just as the poet ceases to be merely "some manly man . . . comic playwright" (507) but instead the defender of justice (510), the sausage-seller ceases to be any man, but instead becomes Senate Victor. Literally, the sausage-seller makes a name for himself. He gives himself an identity. He is no longer merely any man, or the embodiment of the principle of equality. The knights allow the sausage-seller to fight alone in the Senate because just as they will not support just "any comic playwright,"[4] they will not support just any man in the contest yet to happen before Demos. When he returns as Senate Victor, the knights make clear that the sausage-seller is no longer any man:

> Now it is fitting for all to shout for joy (616-7).

The sausage-seller has distinguished himself, and he is therefore worthy of everyone's praise. Although the sausage-seller is merely one of the crowd, he is worthy of the crowd's acclaim. The gentlemanly knights, distinguished for their valor, wealth, birth, and education, are suited to the task of identifying distinction. The plot of the *Knights* has given them a difficult task however. While they require a man of distinct ability if Paphlagon is to be defeated, they require an undistinguished man in order to appeal to Demos, for Demos' city is founded on the principle of equality, and he will never consent to being governed by someone who flouts this principle, or who stands out too much. The knights must choose someone without being un-democratic. But unless one chooses at random, this is impossible. For a non-random choice recognizes distinctions between people, and therefore violates the principle of equality. That is why Demosthenes, as we have seen, "chooses" the first sausage-seller who happens along. And this is why the Senate battle solves the knights' problem well. It enables the knights to ascertain whether the sausage-seller is choiceworthy without seeming to make a choice. The contest will make it for them.

Earlier in the play, Demosthenes, said to be one of Demos' slaves, places his trust in the sausage-seller, in part, it seems because when drunk he allows the oracle to sanction his random selection, and, in part, because he conducts an interview during which he instills in the sausage-seller, or so he believes, the means to defeat Paphlagon (155-235). The knights never consult the oracle. As far as we know, the knights are ignorant as to the oracle's existence and to Demosthenes' preparation of the sausage-seller. Their support of the sausage-seller stems from his success in the Senate, or his deeds. Given the alliance that forms between the sausage-seller, or democratic man, and the knights, or aristocratic men, is Aristophanes suggesting that democratic and aristocratic principles are reconcilable? That is, that democratic principles may take on an elevated form? Or does the alliance suggest the corruption of aristocracy, the debasement of any principle of merit?

After the knights ask the sausage-seller to recount what happened in the Senate, the sausage-seller agrees, saying "indeed the affair is worth hearing" (624). His actions, he believes, are worthy of a public audience. Earlier in the play, however, when the sausage-seller was being interviewed by Demosthenes, he said of himself that he is not even a manly man, let alone a ruler. He does not consider himself worthy to hold great power (178-182). He perfectly embodies the democratic principle. Not only does Demosthenes choose him via the democratic means of choice, the lot—democratic because it allows one to choose without drawing distinctions, the man he chooses by lot also views himself as no better than anyone else. As everyone's equal, he deserves to stand above no one. Now, however, freshly arrived from his first public act, a victory in the Senate, he believes he can make claims on others. He deserves to be heard. In a sense he is democratic man no longer, because he no longer believes he is equal. In another sense, he represents a necessary consequence of democratic equality, its instability or open-endedness. In a city where all are equal, every man is equally deserving of everything, or has an equal right to take all he can get. Any man is eligible to become a ruler or a god, just as lowly Demos has become tyrant of Athens, and roguish Paphlagon has become a god among men.

The sausage-seller begins his narration from the point at which he left the knights and Demosthenes. In beginning from the beginning, his account starts with what the knights know is true, for they saw him race after Paphlagon (498-502). As he says, "[I was] right behind Paphlagon" (624). In the very next moment, according to his account, he is at the gates of the Senate, listening to Paphlagon issuing charges against the knights. According to his narrative, one moment he and Paphlagon are outside the Senate, in the next he is outside, and Paphlagon is in. How did this happen? Was he stopped at the door, while Paphlagon was able to just walk in? Or, did he choose to wait outside? From the very start of his narrative, he makes clear that contrary to the knights' request to hear all (620), the sausage-seller will not say all.

Although the sausage-seller is outside the Senate, he could hear and see the activity occurring inside. He hears Paphlagon Zeus-like hurling thunderous, crashing speeches against the knights; and, he sees the Senators' faces reacting as though they are being persuaded (626-31).[5] According to the sausage-seller, Paphlagon does not include him in his condemnations, only the knights. Before Paphlagon left for the Senate, however, he threatens to bring charges against all present—the knights, the sausage-seller and Demosthenes (475-9). In the parabasis just as the knights in speaking to Athens portray themselves as the selfless defenders of the city (576-80), the sausage-seller in speaking to the knights portrays himself as the selfless defender of the knights.

The sausage-seller, apparently, after seeing that the Senate is being bamboozled by Paphlagon, says he then recited a prayer to his gods to bestow upon him the traits of boldness,[6] a smooth tongue[7] and a shameless voice,[8] that he thinks will be necessary to turn the Senate in his favor (637-8). In order to acquire these traits (all of which Demosthenes had asserted the sausage-seller already possessed), he prays to Lewdness, Fraud, Gullibility, Knavishness, Impudence and Market (634-6). Even including the last, which recalls a smooth tongue and shameless voice, all of the sausage-seller's gods represent low-level vices, which he has turned into virtues by making gods out of them.[9] The sausage-seller's prayer suggests that he is a miniature version of Athens. For just as he converts low-level vices into gods, Athens will convert the sausage-seller, the embodiment of all these vices, into the god-like ruler of Athens. Hyper-democracy deals with its vices not by emphasizing the beauty of virtue, but by blurring the distinction between virtue and vice, so that vices come to be regarded as virtues. If democracy means equality, virtue = vice. Under absolute equality there is no basis for maintaining the distinction between virtue and vice. Why democracy even hangs on to its gods, or its virtues, is not yet clear.

The gods to whom the sausage-seller prays above are invoked, it would seem, because they helped him make a living in the market-place (636). He assumes that they will similarly help him in the Senate. The sausage-seller wants to bring his market gods, who assist him in the realm of self-interest, into the Senate, the realm of the public good. When the sausage-seller hears a man farting on his right, so he says, he interprets it as a response to his prayer. Then, he makes supplications to his gods, forces open the Senate barrier with his ass, and storms in (638-42).

As the sausage-seller enters the Senate on the wings of his prayer to his market gods, it must be mentioned that right before the sausage-seller left for the Senate, the knights say, "may Zeus of public meetings guard you" (499-500).[10] The knights comically associate the sausage-seller, a private man if there ever was one, with public-minded Zeus. In the sausage-seller's narrative, however, as we have just seen above, Zeus shows up not in the sausage-seller's prayer but as the sausage-seller's adversary, for Paphlagon is portrayed as a Zeus-like figure, hurling thunderbolts. But whereas Zeus hurls thunderbolts in order to punish injustice, and thereby supports political life, Paphlagon hurls speeches which lay claim to justice in order to punish his rivals, thereby undermining political life. For Zeus, the thunderbolt is the weapon of justice. For Paphlagon, justice, or punishment, is the weapon of injustice. As defender of justice, and of the public realm, the knights hope that Zeus guards the sausage-seller. Little do they know it is not the sausage-seller who needs to be protected by Zeus, it is Zeus who needs to be protected from the sausage-seller. For the sausage-seller's cure for the sickness ailing the public realm is to get rid of it. In the Senate, the sausage-seller and his gods aim to replace Zeus. Market gods replace the public god.

The difference between the principles of "Zeus agoraios" and the sausage-seller's gods is evident in the sausage-seller's opening statement to the Senate:

> Oh Senate, I am bringing good news, and wish to be first to announce it to you. Since the war burst down on us, I have never seen sardines cheaper (642-45).

The sausage-seller's good news is cheap food. His news is tendered in order to appeal to the most private appetite, the desire for a meal. He caters to the Senator's appetites rather than to their office because he wants to turn the Senators into customers, and the Senate into a mere extension of the market. In making the Senate part of the market he gives himself the home field advantage. The contest with Paphlagon will be fought not over justice, which is Paphlagon's area of expertise, and Zeus' concern, but over satisfying hunger—the sausage-seller's specialty.

After the sausage-seller tells the Senate about the sardines, he tells them "in strict secrecy" that in order to take advantage of the cheapness of sardines, they should quickly take from the market all of the bowls (647-50). His rationale seems to be that if the Senators corner the market in bowls the demand and the price of sardines will drop, because without bowls no one will buy sardines for lack of a container in which to put them. The sausage-seller seems to be not only announcing the existence of cheap sardines, he is engineering it. Whatever he is up to, the Senate shifts his way (651).

The sausage-seller encourages the Senators' self-interest by appealing to their appetites. By making them take an oath of secrecy, he goes one step further. Athens establishes a Senate, in part, because it believes given the opportunity to deliberate over public questions behind closed doors,[11] Senators will not merely defend their own good, but the good of Athens. In giving them a "secret" tip, the sausage-seller wants to drive a wedge between the Senate and Athens, so that even if it hangs on to the notion of a public good, it will give primacy to their own self-interest. The sausage-seller has arranged for all of them to get cheap sardines through buying up all of the bowls. Presumably, without bowls, no one else will be able to get cheap sardines, or any sardines at all. The sausage-seller is making the Senate one hungry body in search of a cheap meal, and to get it they must make sure everyone else goes hungry. The sausage-seller undermines their concern for the public good, by turning this public body into a private body with interests distinct from the rest of Athens.

The sausage-seller gets the Senators to abandon the public good not only by appealing to their appetites. He suggests to them that the public good is not theirs to control. His sardine announcement is worded so as to make it appear that the war just happens. He refers to the war as having come down upon them (644). The sausage-seller's wording is perfectly suited to his strategy of making the Senate passive with respect to the public realm. Since public problems are beyond them, they should concern themselves with their own private problems. Either the sausage-seller's suggestion works so well, or they were so ripe for it that the Senate fails to see that if a cheap meal is what they are after, rather than buy up all the bowls, they should treat the war as of human origin, and move Demos to seek peace. For then the price of sardines and most everything else would drop as markets opened up again and were no longer impinged upon by the war. The private good has so replaced the public good that not even a sense of enlightened self-interest can keep alive their concern about the public good. They are being converted into purely self-interested beings.

According to the sausage-seller, Paphlagon was well aware what was going on and came up with an idea (652-654). Paphlagon proposes to the Senators that they offer a sacrifice of 100 bulls to Athena, in order to thank her for the cheap sardines which the sausage-seller had just reported (654-656). Paphlagon knows that after the sacrifice of the bulls will come the eating of them. So his proposal like the sausage-seller's is targeted at the Senators' appetite. The sausage-seller has succeeded in steering the debate his way. No longer is Paphlagon talking about the anti-Athenian activity of the knights. No longer is he using justice as weapon. He has been lured into a hunger-quenching contest with a seller of food. Paphlagon has not entirely given up his customary manner of argument, however. Although he no longer speaks of Athens and of sins against her, he now speaks of Athena, Athens' patron goddess. By mentioning Athena he offers the Senators a reminder of the holiness of the city, and of their office as defenders of the public good. But if it seems to them that his proposal is public-minded, he is still catering to their desire for a meal. Just as his indictment against the knights was self-interest dressed up as the public good, so is his sacrifice proposal.

Paphlagon's attempt at winning back the Senate is flawed, for he has not shifted the Senators' attention away from their bodies and their hunger. He is still speaking the sausage-seller's language. In fact, by calling in Athena, he sanctifies the sausage-seller's move. He tells the Senate that a cheap meal for them can be cloaked as a public sacrifice. Athena approves their self-interested deliberations. Paphlagon might have brought in the gods to sanctify his own effort to purge Athens of the unjust and conspiratorial knights. Having seen the applause the sausage-seller wins by offering the Senate a meal, he cannot but do the same. Although his proposal swings the Senate back in his direction, his gain is short-lived. For the sausage-seller wins the Senate back merely by accepting Paphlagon's sacrifice proposal but adding to it. He increases the number of bulls to be sacrificed to 200, and adds that 1000 goats be sacrificed to Artemis if anchovies drop in price to 100 an obol. The sausage-seller, realizing that Paphlagon's proposal is of the same currency as his own, makes it his own merely by adding an amendment. The Senate is his for good (657-663).

As the sausage-seller tells it, Paphlagon now becomes temporarily insane. Noise continues to come from his mouth, but it does not make any sense (664). The sausage-seller in subverting the public realm has deprived Paphlagon of speech. "Public" life has been "privatized." There is no way to inflame the Senate over crimes against Athens if the Senate is interested only in satisfying its own hunger. Seeing him in a tizzy, the Senate officers carry Paphlagon towards the exit, as the Senators clamor on about the sardines. Paphlagon's "sputtering" and the senators' "clamor" signal the end of public speech, or public deliberation. Speech is less for the sake of communication, than it is for private gratification.

Paphlagon's senselessness cannot be fully understood unless we more fully understand the revolutionary character of the sausage-seller's amendment to Paphlagon's sacrifice proposal. The sausage-seller proposes that 1000 goats be sacrificed to Artemis if anchovies become cheap. At Marathon, the Athenians promised Artemis a goat for every Persian soldier killed. The Athenians were forced to break their word however, because the excessive number of Persians killed made their promise too expensive. They make Artemis settle for 500 goats. In promising Artemis 1000 goats for inexpensive anchovies, the sausage-seller calculates that cheap fish is worth two Marathons.[12] The sausage-seller suggests that inexpensive food, a private good, something one experiences on one's own, and which does not require the existence of political life let alone Athens, is twice as important as the most glorious victory in Athenian history, its greatest public achievement. The sausage-seller's amendment represents the absolute depreciation of the public, at the same time that it represents the conquest of the private over the public. For not only is the private good of cheap food deemed more valuable than the public good of a military victory. The custom of a public sacrifice which had served the purpose of thanking the gods for public blessings has been taken over by the purpose of thanking them for a private blessing. Moreover, the sacrifices being offered are thinly veiled justifications of pure self-indulgence. Paphlagon is speechless for good reason. Paphlagon is the man who uses justice as a weapon, but justice requires one to recognize the existence of a public good. Paphlagon babbles because it is no use decrying sin to atheists.

Paphlagon is not quite finished, however. Amidst the Senators' uproar over the sardines, he regains his senses, and beseeches them to pause a moment so that he may inform them about the peace terms offered by a Spartan herald (667-69). Paphlagon as he is being carried out the door attempts to revive the Senate's concern for the city and therewith his own standing within the Senate. Despite the fact that his move perfectly exemplifies the Paphlagon way—pursuing his own private good while seeming to pursue a public good—this is one time the Senate should heed his words. Peace at this point in the war would make Athens the strongest city in the Greek world.[13] And, as far as the Senators' appetites are concerned, peace will yield cheap sardines and probably many other commodities as things return to normal. Paphlagon's proposal would enable the Senators to be both good citizens and happy private men. His proposal offers both a public and a private good to them too.

Despite the twofold attractiveness of Paphlagon's proposal, the Senate rejects it. They are too much the converts of the sausage-seller to even consider it properly, as one can see from the sausage-seller's narrative:

> But the Senators from one mouth all cried: "A peace treaty now? Yes, since, my good man, they perceive that our sardines are cheap. We do not want a peace treaty. The war continues!" (670-3).

The sausage-seller has so corrupted the Senate that their sole interest is sardines. Their hunger for sardines leads them to view the Spartan peace offering in terms of sardines, rather than viewing sardines in terms of peace. Peace should be their goal, at least, because it will in time yield cheap sardines. That the Senate is thinking in the way the sausage-seller would hope is the measure of his victory. Their private good, eating cheap sardines and eating them now, has replaced the concern about the public, a concern which, evidently, they used to have, for their faces registered concern when Paphlagon told them about the conspiracy of the knights. Whether the Senators were public-minded or not, they are no longer. For after declaring that the war continues, "they leapt over the railings at every point" and made a dash for the agora (675). The barrier between the Senate and the outside, like the barrier in every human being between self and city, has been obliterated. It can no longer keep the Senators vigilant defenders of the public good just as surely as it cannot keep them within the confines of the Senate. The public good has been abandoned, along with the Senate.

In eliminating Paphlagon from the Senate, whose thunder reminds us of Zeus, and who like Zeus is third generation, the sausage-seller has also eliminated Zeus. In abandoning the Senate, the Senators have abandoned "Zeus agoraios" (of public meetings), for they abandon the public assembly and justice over which Zeus watches. Heading for the open air of the market, the Senators neither fear being struck by an indictment from Paphlagon nor a thunderbolt from Zeus. Zeus has been replaced by the gods to whom the sausage-seller prays before entering the Senate, Lewdness, Fraud, Gullibility, Knavishness, Impudence and Market. The gods of the market now hold sway, as is evident from the behavior of the Senators: they use their public office to pursue private gain, and go to the extreme of allowing a war to continue so that they may buy cheap sardines. These gods render the public realm and justice obsolete. For whereas Zeus punishes injustice, these gods reward it. And whereas Zeus guards public assemblies where citizens may deliberate over the public good, these gods encourage citizens to abandon the public realm in order to pursue their private advantage. In ridding the Senate of Paphlagon, the sausage-seller rids it of injustice, but the price was high. Justice—even Paphlagon's version of it—and the Senate itself have been eliminated.

The change that the sausage-seller provides is from bad to worse. Paphlagon was bad, but the sausage-seller is worse. For although Paphlagon misuses justice, at least he keeps in play the idea of justice and the deliberation this idea requires. Although it was a last-ditch effort to save his own hide, he finally recommends a policy—peace—that is in Athens' best interest. By contrast, the sausage-seller makes further deliberation in the Senate over justice impossible, and therefore justice becomes impossible. The sausage-seller replaces deliberation over justice—albeit a highly flawed version of justice—with knavish scheming in pursuit of a meal. Paphlagon uses the Senate to hammer conspirators; the sausage-seller makes conspirators of the Senate. In turning the instrument for the punishment of conspirators into conspirators, the sausage-seller makes public servants indistinguishable from private actors at the same time he gives everyone license to pursue his own advantage in complete freedom. There is nothing left to supply a constraint. If it is correct to regard the sausage-seller as the angel of absolute equality, the consequence of his rule seems to follow from the idea which he embodies. Absolute equality in leading to the blurring of distinctions between the private and the public leads to the blurring of distinctions between justice and injustice. The consequence of blurring these distinctions is that human beings turn into creatures of appetite. In absolute democracy, the low replaces the high, base gods replaces Zeus, and the human ass replaces Delphi.[14]

The sausage-seller is not without a defense however. In purging "Zeus agoraios" from Athens and replacing him with his market gods, one might argue that he is merely ridding Athens of a god hopelessly in conflict with himself. For that "agora" is in "agoraios" is more than an accident of spelling. Zeus is the god of the market place as well as the public assembly. In that the market place may be regarded as the symbolic representation of the private in that private aims are pursued here, Zeus can be said to sanction both aspects of city life: its propensity for enhancing material well-being, and for enabling human beings to transcend mere materiality. One might argue, however, that Zeus in supporting both aims places human beings in conflict with themselves. His support of material well-being and justice leads to the loss of both, because it is inevitable that a Paphlagon arise to misuse justice, as surely as it is inevitable that the many will dominate and mistakenly give rule to a Paphlagon. When this occurs, city life fails to provide both material well-being and justice. For Paphlagon exploits justice to such a degree he forces his city to punish other cities for their "injustice," unjustly; and, gives rise to wars which make human life nasty, brutish and short. Zeus' support of the public realm, therefore, not only makes impossible a pleasant material existence, but leads to a world of absolute injustice. Perhaps Zeus is the sausage-seller's target after all. In getting rid of Zeus, the sausage-seller makes possible an existence of material sufficiency which Zeus had put in jeopardy.

The elimination of the public by the private that takes place within the sausage-seller's report about his Senate victory also takes place vis a vis the play and us. In presenting us the Senate debate by means of the sausage-seller's narrative, Aristophanes has replaced the drama with the sausage-seller's recollection, the public acting out of the scene with his private account. The consequences for us are the same as they are for the characters within the play. Just as we are totally dependent upon him, and thus have lost our freedom, the freedom we had to view the action of the scene and form our own conclusions, the privatized city of Athens is about to become totally dependent on his rule. Absolute disengagement from public concerns, a complete turn to the private, looks like freedom, but necessarily follows in the loss of freedom.[15]

Notes

1. In addition to the Assembly Athens had a *Boule*, or Senate. Whereas the Assembly was open to all, one had to be selected to attend the Senate. It was therefore less democratic than the Assembly. During the fifth century, as Athens became more democratic, the Senate's power decreased. At the time of the play, as a reading of the play suggests, it seems to have had mostly an advisory role. According to Croiset, Cleon was elected senator in 425, "which made it possible for him to exert a preponderating influence on the the grand council of the republic, which supervised the administration of the navy and that of the treasury, discussed with the generals the measures to be undertaken, and worked out, in advance, all the deliberations of the assembly" (*Aristophanes*, 62). Whatever the case may be in historical Athens, the *Boule* exerts no influence whatsoever upon Demos.

Boule, besides referring to a branch of government may also mean will or purpose. The role Aristophanes assigns the Boule in the play is curiously in line with these definitions. For in the *Knights* the Boule has will and purpose, but it has no power or agency.

2. In the parabasis, the chorus comes forward to address the audience in the poet's name.

3. But, one might argue, perhaps if the sausage-seller had lost in the Senate, he would never have had the opportunity to win in the Assembly. But Demos never asks the sausage-

seller whether he has received the Senate's approval. We are given no reason to believe Demos requires the Senate's approval before acting. Had the sausage-seller lost in the Senate, there is nothing in the play to suggest that he could not have won in the Assembly.

4. The parabasis begins as follows:

> If any comic playwright of old had tried to compel us to come forward to the audience and make a speech, it would have been no easy matter for him to gain his wish (507-9).

Whereas the knights will not choose just anyone, Athenian political life has degenerated to the point where any man will do. The knights are out of place in Athens, and by the end of the play are reduced to irrelevance. The sausage-seller no longer needs them and Demos does not so much as acknowledge them. See 1325-36.

5. In similar fashion, is the sausage-seller reading the faces of the knights?

6. Cf. 181.

7. Cf. 215-6.

8. Cf. 218.

9. *Agora* connotes a public meeting place. It is where one could buy and sell. And it is where public meetings were held. For example, the Assembly was situated in the agora. On the one hand, in that the agora is a place of commerce, it represents the private. On the other hand, in that it is the site of the Assembly, it represents the public. The sausage-seller as a "market" man is moving from selling sausages to rhetoric more generally. This is what it means for him to turn his vices into gods.

10. In Greek, *Zeus agoraios*.

11. Cf. 641, 675. The sausage-seller has to knock down a barrier to get in. In Greek, *kinklis*, or *druphaktos*. Through the sausage-seller's presentation, Aristophanes makes clear that the Senate is separated from the outside by a barrier.

12. See Neil, 98.

13. The sausage-seller has driven Paphlagon to become a peace advocate. As Thucydides tells us, Cleon was notorious for the violence of his character (3.36). Furthermore, it is immediately after Cleon's (and Brasidas') death that we get the peace of Nicias (5.11-13). The sausage-seller's conquest over Paphlagon can be marked by the transformation he forces the violent Paphlagon to undergo.

14. See 638-40, p. 33 above. The sausage-seller assumes that a fart from the man on his right contains a message from above.

15. The focus of our attention in this chapter has been the debate in the Senate. Croiset disposes of this debate in a single paragraph (1909, 80).

CHAPTER FOUR

The End of Demos' Democratization

Whereas the sausage-seller wins the Senate's vote in a single battle, winning over Demos is not so easy. As Demosthenes said earlier, little old man Demos is peevish and grumpy (42). One battle and one obol's worth of coriander are not enough to satisfy Demos (680-2). As tyrant (40, 58, 1114), Demos expects much more and can ask for anything he wants. Given Demos' fickleness and freedom to make extravagant demands, the chief servant's tenure seems destined to be short. The moment Demos craves something which the chief servant cannot deliver he is likely to be replaced. The trick to remaining chief servant may be, not to give Demos what he wants, but to make Demos want what one is capable of giving. Remaining in power, then, as Demos' chief servant, requires that one become his superior. But how is one to achieve superiority over Demos in the regime of absolute equality over which Demos himself presides? The chief servant cannot, like a doctor, just tell Demos that he knows better what is good for him, for Demos may find such assertions of superior knowledge insulting and undemocratic.[1] Pericles is dead. Demos will no longer submit to reason.[2]

As Aristophanes suggests, the tyranny of absolute equality drives knowledge underground. Boasts about one's knowledge are no longer safe to make in public. Paphlagon's own boasts about his knowledge are always made behind Demos' back, never to his face.[3] As servant to Demos, one can afford neither to write Demos a blank check, nor to check Demos' desires with assertions of superior wisdom. So, how is one to keep in Demos' favor?

If Aristophanes' presentation of the Paphlagon-sausage-seller fight is our guide, the way to manage Demos is to induce him to fall in love with you. In the first battle for Demos' hand, Paphlagon presents himself as Demos' lover and tries to arouse his love. He attempts to become Demos' beloved. If he becomes Demos' beloved, Demos becomes his servant rather than the other way around.

By offering himself to Demos as a love candidate, however, Paphlagon unknowingly shifts the basis of the contest from economics to beauty. Demos may marry for economic reasons, but only beauty sweeps him off his feet. Paphlagon claims to know Demos' stomach (715), but does he know his heart? What does it mean to know the heart of Demos?

Because forcing Demos into love—rape—does not seem possible, in order to win the love of Demos, the two candidates will have to offer Demos a love speech, a reason why each ought to be loved. Each will attempt to supply the most appealing account possible of what he represents. Each will make known his virtues, and in so doing makes known the future in store for Demos. The virtue that Demos will try to make its own is whichever of these two warring accounts of virtue Demos falls for. Eros induces the lover to lose himself in his beloved. Whereas Demos may find the doctor's speech obnoxious because of its presumption of superiority, Demos approves of the superiority embedded in the love speech, because he longs to unite with it, and make it his own.

In this chapter, we shall examine the contest between Paphlagon and the sausage-seller for Demos' love. That contest is prepared by the sausage-seller's announcing to the chorus the news of his victory in the Senate. After the Chorus' song of praise and encouragement (683-90), Paphlagon reappears. His reappearance is announced by the sausage-seller in sarcastic terms (691-3).[4] The humor Paphlagon now arouses in the sausage-seller contrasts sharply with the fear Paphlagon aroused in him at first (240-1). Before, Paphlagon made him run. Now, he makes him laugh. Similarly, the terror Paphlagon projects contrasts sharply with the sausage-seller's mockery. He mocks each of Paphlagon's six successive threats (694-711). Despite the knights' warning about the battle yet to be fought (687-88), the sausage-seller is loose as a goose.[5]

The sausage-seller's amazing transformation is in keeping with democracy's necessary belief that any man can become anything. A coward can become a he-man (457), and a sausage-seller can become a Senate Victor.[6] Absolute democracy recognizes no limit to what any man can become, therefore the confidence, even boldness, of the sausage-seller is fitting. After all, he has just given himself the name "Senate Victor." In his boldness he is quintessentially democratic, and, because this Athens is an absolute democracy, he is also quintessentially Athenian. His accomplishments mimic those of Athens. Like Athens during the Persian war, he abandoned his possessions and turf (488-9) to meet his enemy in a battle (490-7) and returned home a hero to a hero's welcome (683-90). He is the new Themistocles (884-6). Except that whereas Themistocles ushered in an era of public-spirited democracy, culminating in Pericles,[7] the sausage-seller completes the move that began with Paphlagon towards a private-spirited democracy.[8] Themistoclean Demos abandoned everything private for the good of the city. The sausage-seller's Demos will abandon everything political for the good of himself (805-11).

Of the sausage-seller's gibes, the one which most riles Paphlagon mentions the loss of his political stature (703-6). Paphlagon cannot stand the thought of becoming equal.[9] Paphlagon's acquired inequality is the compromise that Demos has had to endure in order to become the proclaimed or nominal master of the city. For Demos' defects make it impossible for him to rule on his own (40-3), and roguish Paphlagon would not serve Demos unless there was something in it for him (1217-23). Here, Paphlagon's threats against the sausage-seller, and the intimidation he was said to practice against his adversaries (58-70), are his way of preserving his inequality. Paphlagon's fear tactics do not seem to fit Athens' current regime, however, as well as the sausage-seller's mockery. Mockery pokes fun at an inequality, usually, as in this case, of a superior, thereby cutting him down to size. Fearmongering requires inequality, for the fearmonger needs superiority in order to induce fear, and preserves inequality, for hurting another makes one relatively stronger. Therefore, Paphlagon's tactics in premise and effect are undemocratic.

Although undemocratic, Paphlagon's tactics and the benefits he derives from them seem to stem from hyper democracy itself. For not only does Demos tolerate the unscrupulousness of his servants as long as he is fed and bathed, but Demos' desire to be ruled by someone like him results in a competitive struggle for power among equals.[10] The political climate is such that Paphlagon cannot be much better than the other servants, so there is always someone almost as good, or bad, ready to seize power (58-60). In order to protect himself, and in order to govern, Paphlagon terrorizes his competition. Without this, he would be forever fending off his rivals and would have no time to rest (102-4) or to tend to Athens' affairs. His fearmongering and greed give him the inequality that nature seems to have deprived him. His ill-gotten superior strength provides him stability, a necessity for executing Demos' government. However, the more his fearmongering and greed succeed, the more he fails, for the stronger he becomes, the more he violates the principle of his regime. Demos' rejection of Paphlagon symbolizes the self-contradiction within democracy (1215-23). In order for democracy to work, it requires the service of inequality.

As Paphlagon's threat against the sausage-seller makes clear, Demos' laissez-faire attitude towards the conduct of his servants and Paphlagon's unscrupulousness threaten to undermine the city:

> I'll drag you to the people, in order that you may pay me justice (710).

For Paphlagon, justice does not represent a collective good. It represents a private good. He exploits the city's appreciation of justice to maintain his own standing in the city. He uses justice as a weapon against his enemies. The base men that Demos allows to serve him debase justice and the city, which without justice is indistinguishable from a band of thieves. Because absolute democracy vests absolutely base men with political power, in absolute democracy righteous vindictiveness replaces justice.[11] The low replaces the high. Paphlagon embodies this tendency.[12]

In response to Paphlagon's threat, the sausage-seller boasts that he will outdo Paphlagon in a battle of demagoguery (711). As Demosthenes said (46-70), Paphlagon considers himself to be the demagogue par excellence, and so he mocks the sausage-seller's demagogic pretensions:

> But, miserable wretch, he's not convinced by anything of yours, but I laugh at him [Demos] as much as I wish (712-3).

Although Paphlagon predicts that the sausage-seller will not be able to persuade Demos, he never refers to his own oratorical skill, or gifts of persuasion. According to Paphlagon's self-understanding, it is not his oratory, or prudence, which distinguishes him, it is the fact that he can say anything to Demos and get away with it. He is beyond reproach. Paphlagon's ability to mock Demos with impunity is the measure of his closeness with Demos. Paphlagon assumes that, because he caters to Demos' whims and because he is similarly base, he has Demos in his back pocket. Therefore, he thinks that he can mock, or chastise, Demos without incurring Demos' wrath, and he cannot imagine another sharing a greater affiliation with Demos.[13] How do Paphlagon's two defining traits fit together? What is the relationship between his self-righteousness and his supposed closeness to Demos?

The rule of Demos represents the rule of the common or base, which plays right into the hands of Paphlagon. Demos listens to Paphlagon, and allows himself to be chastised by him, not because he trusts in Paphlagon's wisdom and character as the people did with Pericles,[14] but because Paphlagon is one of them. Pericles idealizes Athenian ways in order to induce the people to embrace them, so that Athens and the Athenians may realize their potential as city and citizens. For Pericles, Athenians are to love Athens not only because they are born in Athens, but because of what Athens represents, as he defines it in his funeral oration.[15] For Paphlagon, Demos should love Paphlagon because he is like them. For Pericles, to be a citizen is to love an ideal. For Paphlagon, to be a citizen is to love your own. If the mark of the political is to be open to the distinction between one's own and justice, under Paphlagon Athens would become more a tribe than a city.[16]

The sausage-seller is struck by Paphlagon's hubris:

> How absolutely convinced you are that the Demos is yours! (714).

The sausage-seller's indignation reminds us that he is the one with the base, demos-like, rearing, not Paphlagon.[17] Therefore, Paphlagon should not be so confident. Attempting to justify his confidence, Paphlagon responds:

For I know with what foods he is fed (715).

Paphlagon believes that his affiliation with Demos gives him superior knowledge of Demos' appetites. Like the mistake he made in the Senate, he is about to engage a food-seller in a cook-off. But here his mistake is greater, for judge-Demos is likely to have a palate more akin to the sausage-seller's than to Paphlagon's.

Rather than refer to his own cooking knowledge, the sausage-seller takes the moral high ground:

> Indeed, just like the nurses, you feed him badly. Chewing his food, you put in his mouth a little, after you've swallowed three times more than he (716-9).

As the man chosen randomly from amidst the crowd, the sausage-seller takes the crowd's point of view. He does not dispute Paphlagon's suggestion that the demagogue should feed the people, just as a nurse feeds a child placed in her care, or as a grown daughter tends to her senile father. Rather, he suggests, that Paphlagon is a bad nurse, because he feeds his charge scraps only after quenching his own appetite. Indeed, he knows "with what foods he is fed," for Paphlagon eats most of it himself. Thus, the sausage-seller suggests that Paphlagon's affiliation with Demos is not strong enough. He behaves like a mercenary nurse. Paphlagon feeds his charge, but he is in it only for the money. He is not truly devoted, unlike the sausage-seller, who when it comes time to call upon Demos addresses him as "father."[18]

Paphlagon, far from denying the sausage-seller's accusation, simply boasts,

> Yes, by Zeus, by my cleverness I am able to make the people wide and narrow (719-20).

Whatever it means to make the people "wide and narrow,"[19] Paphlagon speaks as vaguely as an oracle. His boast reveals his arrogance for he claims god-like power over the people's size. His wizardry thus allows him to steal food from Demos' mouth, because he not only knows Demos' appetites, he controls Demos' size.

In boasting about his control of the people, Paphlagon swears by Zeus, but once again he seems to defile Zeus rather than carry out his mission. In the Senate, the lightning flashes of Paphlagon's indictments defend his interests, not the city's, not justice. Zeus defends justice; Paphlagon subverts it. Here, he boasts to give Demos his very shape. When Zeus gave human beings their shape, according to the speech Plato attributes to Aristophanes in the *Symposium*, Zeus split them into two, giving them a yearning for something more complete than themselves.

Paphlagon simply makes Demos wide and narrow. His manipulation of Demos' size makes Demos dependent on him, who while cheating Demos instills in Demos the belief that Demos' self-interest is all that matters. Zeus enables man to look beyond himself. Paphlagon induces Demos to focus only on himself by representing justice as self-interest (873-4).[20]

The sausage-seller is not impressed by Paphlagon's boast that he can make the people wide and narrow. He says it is no more impressive that his control over his own behind:

> My own ass too is wise in that (721).

In being able to manipulate Demos, Paphlagon likens himself to a god. The sausage-seller's wisecrack suggests that if Demos is a mere extension of Paphlagon, if his popularity is rooted in his affiliation, in nothing else, then his success with Demos is not more elevated than one's control over one's own body parts, and a base body part at that. Despite the truth in the sausage-seller's joke, it obscures more than it reveals. As the representative of the private realm, the sausage-seller cannot be expected to understand Paphlagon's perverse effect upon Athenian political life. Not only does Paphlagon subvert justice by making it serve his own self-interest. In contrast with Pericles, who depicted the city as the vehicle by which all citizens may become virtuous, and therefore free, Paphlagon makes the city the vehicle by which he becomes free, while everyone else becomes his slave.

With both contestants confident in their own demagoguery, both summon Demos from inside his home. At first, Demos tries to shoo his visitors away, despite Paphlagon's complaint about being abused. Then, reluctantly, Demos answers his door, and asks Paphlagon, "who wrongs you?"[21] (728-730). Unlike Paphlagon, who immediately upon storming out from Demos' house earlier (235-39) smells conspiracy afoot, resembling the dog to which he is likened (1014-1020, 1023, 1030), Demos has no idea what is going on. He seems completely ignorant of the noisy political struggle taking place right outside his front door. Although Demos is tyrant of Athens, and as such is the most political being, for almost one half the play Demos remains at home—and offstage. Because the adjudication of the present case supplies the content of the rest of the play, and Demos is called to judge, Demos will now remain in the public realm. The split occurring in the play between Demos at home (1-727) and Demos in the public realm (728-1408) mirrors the split within Demos himself, between his private disposition and his political function: Demos adjudicates cases, but only for pay; and, he takes part in political deliberations, but makes them serve his private needs (50-52, 797-800, 1121-30). Given Demos' self-interestedness, one might say that this split is purely cosmetic. Even in the political realm, Demos behaves as if he were at home. Nevertheless, one can summarize the plot of the *Knights* as follows: Paphlagon needs to maintain this split, as we shall see, while the sausage-seller needs to make it disappear. With the death of the Senate, Paphlagon's continued reign depends more than ever on the continued political participation of "stupid-faced Demos" (395-6).

Responding to Demos' question as to who is wronging him, Paphlagon says:

> On account of you I am being beaten by this one [the sausage-seller] and these young ones [the knights] (730-1).

Paphlagon was asked, "who . . . ," but responds first with why, and only then with who. He is beaten because of Demos. He wants Demos to believe that a slap at Paphlagon is a slap at Demos. His assailants are Demos' assailants. For he is Demos' man, while his assailants are upper-class. Rather than recall the fact that his adversary was reared on dog food (411-16), Paphlagon emphasizes the sausage-seller's association with the upper-class knights, so as to prejudice Demos against the sausage-seller.

Apparently, Paphlagon's answer intrigues Demos, for he asks for more explanation as to why he is being beaten (731). Paphlagon responds:

> Because I love you, Oh Demos, and because I am your lover (731).

Behind Demos' back Paphlagon said, as we saw, that he is a Demos-manipulator. In front of Demos, he is a Demos-lover. But he is still trying to manipulate Demos. His move here resembles the move he attempted on the knights. There, he tried to win the knights' approval by offering them a monument to courage (266-72), the virtue to which the knights are devoted (565-581, 595-611). Here, he tries to win Demos' approval by offering Demos what Demos most desires—complete devotion to himself.

Although Paphlagon's monument proposal is intended as a bribe, had the knights accepted it, and had Paphlagon delivered, his monument would have served as testimony to the city's love of courage, thereby shedding luster on the life of virtue. In dealing with Demos, Paphlagon cannot offer Demos a testimonial to virtue, because Demos is without virtue. The despotism of Demos symbolizes the rule of the common or base. Since Demos is virtue-less, Paphlagon attempts to endear himself to Demos by creating a virtue and convincing Demos that he embodies it. Paphlagon says he "loves" Demos, and is his "lover." As Paphlagon moves from the verb, "love," to the noun, "lover," he transforms the act, loving Demos, into a virtue, Demos-lover. As Demos-lover, Paphlagon is the monument upon which Demos should fix his adoring eyes, because Paphlagon fixes his adoring eyes upon Demos. The lover deserves to become beloved simply because of his love. In dealing with the knights, he offers them a symbol embodying that for which the knights strive and which they love—manliness. In dealing with Demos, he offers himself to Demos as the symbol of that for which Demos strives and which he loves—being loved. By projecting himself as Demos-lover, Paphlagon appeals to Demos' necessary belief in his own inherent worth or lovability. Demos wants to be loved because he exists. The fact that Demos is without real excellence is besides the point. Real excellence has no place in an absolute democracy. By creating the virtue, "Demos-lover," Paphlagon tells Demos he has a right to be loved. At the same time, he justifies his flattery of Demos, and suggests that the sausage-seller opposes this democratic right.

After Paphlagon's explanation, Demos now moves to give equal time to the sausage-seller, asking, "who are you?" (733). Like Paphlagon, he chooses to answer a different question. He tells Demos not who he is, but what he represents. He says nothing about his profession or his rearing in the market. He calls himself Paphlagon's "rival-lover" for Demos' heart, and declares "that he has been loving Demos a long time and has been desiring to do some good for Demos" (733-34). Then, in a surprise move, he accepts Paphlagon's association of him with the aristocratic knights and then identifies Paphlagon as among the base (continuing from above):

> and many others both beautiful and good. But we are not able to on account of that guy. You are like the boys who have lovers. You do not accept the beautiful and good, you offer yourself to lampsellers and cobblers and shoemakers and leather-sellers (735-40).

Up until this point, one can say that the sausage-seller faithfully executes the plan of Demosthenes. For example, before entering the Senate, he calls upon the very qualities that Demosthenes said were necessary.[22] Here, however, he breaks from Demosthenes' plan, and charts his own course. Demosthenes asserted that the sausage-seller's lack of education and gentlemanly upbringing is an advantage (178-188). Here, for the moment, they have become a disadvantage. He wants to be regarded as one of the beautiful and good. The sausage-seller audaciously suggests that he is not the sleazy salesman, Paphlagon is, and that Paphlagon's love-overtures threaten to turn Demos into a slut. The sausage-seller wants to give Demos back his respectability. Might the sausage-seller represent a nobler alternative to Paphlagon, contrary to what we had assumed? Or is his appeal to the noble and the good a surer means to success than Paphlagon uses?

Whereas Paphlagon attempts to endear himself to Demos by catering to Demos' self-love, the sausage-seller attempts to endear himself to Demos by dressing himself up as beautiful. The sausage-seller debases Paphlagon by portraying him as a mercenary lover, believing his gifts compensate for his ugliness.

And, he shames Demos for choosing gift-bearers over the beautiful and good. Paphlagon, in turn, defends himself by saying that he "does good for Demos" (741). In defending himself, in effect, Paphlagon confesses his guilt. He admits to buying Demos' love with goods. Paphlagon wants a love-affair based on the mutual satisfaction of interests.

In spite of his appeal to the noble over the mercenary, the sausage-seller admits that he too wishes to give Demos gifts (734), and demands that Paphlagon reveal the good he does Demos (741). In order to prove his benevolence, Paphlagon mentions his success at Pylos:

> Deceiving the generals on Pylos, I sailed there and brought back the Laconians (742-3).

Paphlagon's success at Pylos caused Sparta to sue for peace. Had Athens accepted, her political future would have looked bright. Although Paphlagon's success may have been due more to luck than skill, his victory is indeed a good for Athens, and therefore for Demos.

According to the sausage-seller, however, it is a trifle:

> And, I taking a walk, stole someone else's pot from the shop as it was boiling (744-45).

The sausage-seller compares Paphlagon's military victory with his own stealing of someone else's food. His comparison has some merit. If it were not for the generalship of Demosthenes, the Laconians would not have been trapped at Pylos for Paphlagon to bring home. At Pylos, Paphlagon exploited an opportunity created by someone else. But while Paphlagon may have stolen an opportunity, his take was much more than "a pot on the boil." His take may have led to the realization of Athenian imperial dreams (797-9, 1011-3, 1086-7). The sausage-seller completely abstracts from the political significance of Paphlagon's theft. Paphlagon stole a meal prepared by someone else,[23] which, according to the sausage-seller's earlier remark, he too is able to do.[24]

Now, Paphlagon is filled with righteous indignation. He demands that Demos hold an Assembly at once. The controversy unfolding before our eyes illustrates Paphlagon's method: make an indictment, then call for a trial. It never fails him, because Demos is persuaded more by the speaker and his bribes than the speech. No one is as low as Paphlagon or will sink to Paphlagon's depths, so Paphlagon always wins (1340-4, 1356-61). Paphlagon's baseness, his hold over Demos and his love of power mean that the wheels of justice are always turning. By keeping them turning, Paphlagon hurts his enemies and feeds Demos. Paphlagon brings the political into every nook and cranny of Athens in order to convert his enemies into a meal for Demos. With self-righteousness, Paphlagon eliminates his enemies and Demos gets a meal (255-57, 977-84). Moreover, in this fashion, he shows Demos the benefits of politics, and thereby maintains Demos' interest in politics. Without a politically interested Demos, Paphlagon's self-righteousness would not work, because only base Demos can be bribed without fail. And, because base Demos can be bribed, because Demos is selfish, Paphlagon instigates controversy wherever he can. Thus, at one and the same time, Paphlagon makes the people more private, because he constantly caters to their self-interest, while making everything else more public, because he constantly issues lawsuits. But, since everything which Paphlagon makes public he gives to the people, excepting that which he retains for himself, the public vanishes in all but in name. Again, absolute democracy generates the equation: the public = the private. In an absolute democracy, the people speak about private goods as if they were public goods. They cannot tell the difference.[25]

Paphlagon, in calling for an Assembly, thinks a change in venue will enable him to finally do away with the sausage-seller, and his wisecracks. What he requires, however, is a change in Demos. The sausage-seller's flippant comparison of the Spartans at Pylos to a stolen meal reveals a chink in Paphlagon's armor. Paphlagon thinks his Pylos success is manifest proof of his goodness to Demos. Is it? How can Paphlagon distinguish his Pylos success from the sausage-seller's comparison? As chief servant, Paphlagon caters to Demos' desire to have politics serve his private needs. This means that politics no longer enables or represents man's ability to transcend self-interest. In political life, Demos does not put aside his appetite for the sake of right, he puts aside right for the sake of his appetite. Paphlagon wants to lure Demos into supporting the political realm and his empire-building by appealing to Demos' private appetites. The sausage-seller wants to show Demos that Paphlagon's political realm and empire-building: (1) requires Demos to sacrifice certain private goods; and (2), is not necessary if all Demos is after is the satisfaction of private desire. Paphlagon would like Demos to regard political life and empire as superior to the life of consumption without political life, but the reign of absolute equality that spawned his political career and which he has supported, leaves him with no basis for establishing this superiority.

Paphlagon wants Demos to hold an Assembly at once,

> so that you may see which of us is more devoted to you, judge between us, in order that you love that one (746-7).

Paphlagon proposes a love affair based completely on the good and not at all upon the noble or beautiful. For his proposal asks that Demos love whoever is devoted to him, or serves Demos' interests. Paphlagon wants Demos to choose a leader by considering only his own private self-interest, not beauty, not principle, and then loving that leader in return. Paphlagon's proposal promotes the idea that all love is self-love. It is the same with choosing a leader as it is with deciding on policy or with rendering a verdict. Despite the fact that Demos deliberates in the Assembly, the public realm, Paphlagon suggests to Demos that he should consider only himself, only his private good. To the extent Demos thinks about justice, it is only a pretty costume covering self-interest. No other justice is in sight. The regime of absolute equality drives justice into equality with self-interest. In the love affair that Paphlagon offers Demos, there is no longing for justice, for the beautiful, or something outside the self which is better than the self. Since only the self is in sight, in politics Demos never rises above himself. Therefore, under Paphlagon, political life does not educate, it corrupts. The eventual ascendance to power of the sausage-seller represents the fulfillment of Demos' corruption, to which Paphlagon has been contributing. In corrupting Demos, Paphlagon sows the seeds of his own destruction.

The sausage-seller echoes Paphlagon's request, with a qualification:

> Yes, Yes, certainly judge, except not on the Pnyx (749).

Whereas Paphlagon encourages Demos to exercise political power by summoning him to the Pnyx, the sausage-seller wants to keep him in the private realm, away from politics. Paphlagon's reign depends upon the continued political interestedness of Demos, and on Demos' continued baseness and stupidity (395-6). If Demos abdicates his throne, if he becomes thoroughly private, Paphlagon's political career is over. For only Demos is base enough to put his love up for sale. Without Demos as his juror Paphlagon would not win his cases.

Demos denies the sausage-seller's request. He spiritedly refuses to sit anywhere but the Pnyx, and exhorts all present and himself to head there (750-1). The sausage-seller is distressed:

> Oh, no, I'm a helpless wretch, I am finished. For the old man at home is the smartest of men, but when he sits on that rock, he gapes like a fig-stringer (752-5).

Despite the fact that in the Assembly, Paphlagon caters to Demos' self-interest, the sausage-seller believes Demos to be a different man there than he is at home. In the Assembly, Demos is self-interested, but, evidently, not self-interested enough. In the Assembly, Paphlagon pulls the wool over Demos' eyes. He portrays his service to Demos as being for Demos' good, but it is only phony goods that Paphlagon delivers. In the Assembly, in the political realm, Paphlagon is able to seduce Demos with political abstractions, like "empire," and "judging." This is exemplified by Demos' own unwillingness to make a decision anywhere but the

Pnyx. The sausage-seller has to make Demos see that Paphlagon's abstractions are nothing compared to what he has to offer, the pleasures of food and sex. The Pnyx is just a rock. Political life is a sham.

Paphlagon opens things in the Assembly with a prayer:

> To *despoine*[26] Athena the ruler of the city I pray, that if I have become the best man for the demos of the Athenians, next to Lysicles, Cynna and Salabacco, just like now for having done nothing, may I dine in the Prytaneum (763-6).

A moment ago, Paphlagon demanded that Demos immediately hold an Assembly. His appeal was to Demos. Once in the Assembly, his appeal is to the goddess Athena. Suddenly, Athens is no longer ruled by *despotes* Demos. It is ruled by *despoina* Athena. The Pnyx is more than a rock, because the earth on which it sits is not just earth. It is earth made holy by Athena. It is a city, and a city require laws, assemblies, and judgements. Because the connection between these political phenomena and Demos' self-interest is not perfectly manifest, Paphlagon hauls Athena into court to give them significance. Paphlagon exploits Demos' religiosity. He uses immanifest Athena to make the immanifest good of the city manifest.

Paphlagon calls upon Athena to reward him if he is the best man to Demos. Thus, being the best man to Demos is to be a just man, for Athena is the goddess of Athens as a whole, and by praying to Athena, Paphlagon implies that he is just.[27] Paphlagon suggests that Athena sanctions the democratic equation, justice = Demos' self-interest. As a reward for being the best man to Demos, for being a good citizen, Paphlagon asks Athena for a public gift: receiving public meals, just as he has been doing (280-3). Paphlagon's prayer is worded so that one may conclude that if everything stays the same, if Paphlagon continues in his current position, Athena has spoken. Paphlagon exploits Athena, or Demos' religiosity, to make Demos believe that he has special political significance. He embodies democratic virtue: being "best man to Demos." In being able to recognize this virtue in Lysicles (a deceased general), and Cynna and Salabacco (prostitutes), Paphlagon lends credibility to the existence of this virtue. The virtue exists, for others possess it too. And, by mentioning these others as examples, Paphlagon gives content to this virtue. Being best man to Demos means servicing Demos, therefore politicians and prostitutes exemplify it. The democratic virtue is open to both genders. Even a woman can be a best man. Paphlagon may be a mercenary lover, but this is what the job description calls for.

The first half of Paphlagon's prayer helps us understand why it behooves the demagogue to be self-righteous. To keep Demos involved in politics, Paphlagon reminds Demos of the holiness of the city: Athena rules Athens, Athena rewards the just man with a public honor. In the midst of Paphlagon's self-interested argument, i.e., his injustice, Paphlagon needs more than ever to maintain the piety of justice. He needs to support justice, in name, in order to continue being unjust, in deed. For if Demos stopped believing in justice, it would not be long before Demos stopped holding trials or stopped participating in politics. Yes, Paphlagon pays Demos for his political participation, but money is a private good, and if Demos wants private goods, Demos may be persuaded that the public realm is expendable. Demos may come to believe that his enjoyment of the private does not require the public.

In the second half of his prayer, Paphlagon defines injustice:

> but if I hate you and on your behalf I alone do not fight standing firm,
> may I be destroyed (767-8).

Deserving punishment, or being unjust means hating Demos. Paphlagon implies, moreover, that there is only one man that fights for Demos. Everyone else is anti-Demos. By giving religious sanction to the notion that only one man fights for Demos, and that those who do not fight for Demos hate Demos, Paphlagon hopes to unleash Demos' fury on those who oppose this one man. For those who oppose this one man not only oppose Demos, they oppose the gods. Moreover, since Paphlagon fully expects that Demos will decide that he is this one man, that he is the Demos-defender, not one of the many Demos-haters, the punishment that Paphlagon asks to receive if he fails the test is the punishment that Paphlagon would lead Demos to impose on his enemies, or on the sausage-seller. That Paphlagon is trying to goad Demos into brutalizing the sausage-seller, once Demos judges in Paphlagon's favor, is apparent in that in the punishment half of his prayer, Paphlagon addresses Demos. When speaking about the reward for the just man Paphlagon addresses Athena, "to despoine Athena . . . I pray, if concerning the people . . . I have been the best man." The people is mentioned only in the third person. However, when speaking about the harsh penalty for the unjust man, Paphlagon speaks directly to Demos, "but if I hate *you* and on *your* behalf I alone standing firm" (my emphasis). When he wants grace, Paphlagon addresses the Goddess. When he wants brutality, he addresses the people.

In one breath, Paphlagon gives a religious sanction to the city; in the next, he takes away the city's value. For he turns citizens into violent brutes, and he makes it impossible for the city to be just. Justice requires citizens to weigh the pros and cons, and therefore requires citizens to be free to exchange speeches. In Paphlagon's Athens, who would dare make a speech when the penalty for doing so may be "being sawn in two, and cut up for yoke straps" (768)?

According to Paphlagon's prayer, Athena rules Athens; but, his prayer notwithstanding, Athena is nowhere. Paphlagon, however, is everywhere (74-79). On Earth, Paphlagon substitutes for Athena. In being everywhere, in defending the political realm, in making apparent that he is the best man to Demos, Paphlagon is merely serving Athena. And, therefore, as Athena's servant, he properly asks Athena for a prize. In bringing in Athena, Paphlagon hopes to sanctify the political realm and his own place as demagogue in Athens. With his talk about Athena, Paphlagon hopes that Demos sees a political halo hovering over his head, so that Demos will fall in love with both the halo—i.e., the political—and the head over which it hovers.

After Paphlagon finishes his prayer, the sausage-seller makes one that on its surface resembles Paphlagon's:

> And may I, oh Demos, if I do not love and cherish [*stergo*] you, be cut up and boiled with mincemeat. And if you do not trust that, on top of this may I be cut up in a mash with cheese[28] (769-71).

The sausage-seller, like Paphlagon, suggests that he is Demos' man for he offers his own life as collateral in support of this claim. However, whereas Paphlagon's prayer is to the goddess, the sausage-seller's never mentions the goddess or any divinity. Nor does the sausage-seller mention the political. The city never comes up. Instead he emphasizes the strength of his love for Demos. Earlier, he addressed Demos as father (725). Now, he calls to Demos' attention his son-like love for Demos.[29] "Stergo" means not only to love, but to love in the way a son loves a father. The sausage-seller in saying that he loves Demos as a son, wants Demos to view him as a son. For he will look out for his father Demos just as a son would. He can be trusted. Moreover, since the son is a product of the father, he resembles the father. And, so just as the son knows how to please himself, a son also knows how to please his father. Therefore, the sausage-seller is not only the most faithful servant, but also the most competent servant.

Paphlagon wants Demos to see him as embodying the democratic takeover of politics: Paphlagon brings the exalted goods of the city down to Demos. The sausage-seller wants Demos to see him as embodying Demos' own flesh and blood: the sausage-seller reacquaints Demos with his own true self. The sausage-seller = Demos—Demos' own political illusions. Strip Demos of the illusions with which Paphlagon and others have clothed him, and Demos would be exactly like the sausage-seller—a thoroughly base man, who is all appetite and no honor, all private and no public. The sausage-seller would like to teach Demos that in maintaining the distinction between the public and private, in refusing to sit anywhere but the Pnyx, Demos is in violation of his own principle. Demos is still in need of democratization. For by maintaining the distinction between the public and the private, Demos recognizes an inequality. And, the distinction which he maintains encouraged by Paphlagon out of self-interest causes him to forego his own good. Demos is forced to adjudicate cases on a hard rock, when he could be having a good time. Demos is deluded. His happiness depends on private not public things. Although Demos is tyrant, his delusions forestall his absolute freedom.

Contrary, then, to Paphlagon's prayer, Paphlagon is not the best man to Demos. For Paphlagon defends the political, and the political, to the extent that it is good, is only an intermediate good. Paphlagon uses the political realm to feed Demos. But, Demos craves neither Paphlagon nor the political. Demos craves food. Demos wants his appetites satisfied. Paphlagon may provide Demos with a meal, indirectly, by pursuing policies that result in more pay and therefore more food for Demos, but he also forces Demos to listen to his speeches. The sausage-seller will offer him food, and more, while closing down the courts (1316-18, 1373-83, 1384-91).

Paphlagon responds by pressing his case that he loves Demos. He shows Demos the meaning of being "best man to Demos":

> And how could there be a citizen, Oh Demos, loving you more than I? First when I was a Senator, I produced for you a great profit in the common reserve, some men I tortured, some I choked, and demanding a share of others, not caring for anyone of the private people, if you I could gratify (773-76).

Paphlagon suggests that although the sausage-seller portrays himself as a son, he is merely another citizen, who cannot possibly love Demos more than Paphlagon. For as Demos' political servant in the Senate, Paphlagon subordinated everything to the city's and therefore Demos' good. Whereas laws exist, in part, to protect human beings and property, Paphlagon makes every private individual and all property subordinate to his novel notion of right, that whatever is good for Demos is just. With Paphlagon at the helm, as long as a state act serves Demos' interests, it receives the rubber stamp of justice. Paphlagon's new right keeps him in power because it enables Demos to profit from gross injustice while believing himself just. Through Paphlagon, Demos gets the material benefits of tyranny and the honor of acting in accordance with justice. Paphlagon enables Demos to live the life of sin, while thinking himself a saint.

Paphlagon suggests that his defense of the "common reserve" proves he loves the people. For whatever belongs to the common belongs to the people. By feeding the common reserve through taxing individual Athenians, Paphlagon claims to gratify Demos. In making this argument, Paphlagon attempts to exploit Demos' naivete. For contrary to Paphlagon's supposition, treasury balances may not be a good measure of the city's health, or even of its wealth, but since treasury balances can be reduced to a simple number, it is a useful demagogic tool. When treasury balances are high, Athens is a healthy city, when they are low, it is sick. Just as seductive is Paphlagon's notion of democratic service. Service to Demos means subordinating everything private to the common or public. Being loyal to Demos and the public means having nothing of your own. It seems Demos is the only one permitted private pleasures. Everyone else must be willing to sacrifice for the public good. Aristophanes' play suggests that in an absolute democracy, the people are the least public-minded, because the people care only about their own appetites. Everything they do is for themselves not the city.

In casting himself as the greatest patriot, Paphlagon radicalizes the split between the public and the private. On the one hand, he produces a great surplus in the common reserve, and, on the other, he oppresses all private individuals. Paphlagon is forced into making this move because of the fact that the sausage-seller fights under the banner of the private. But there really is nothing public, or common, about the good Paphlagon supplies the people. For the gratification which Paphlagon says he delivers the people is private in character (50-2). There are no public goods, only private goods. Paphlagon's self-defense is contradictory, as the sausage-seller is about to show.

Whereas Paphlagon casts himself as the greatest patriot, the sausage-seller casts him as a mere thief. To Paphlagon's claim that he squeezed others for Demos' sake, the sausage-seller responds:

> Oh Demos, there is nothing august[30] in that. I'll do that for you too. Grabbing other people's bread, I'll serve it to you (777-78).

Paphlagon depicts himself as the ideal public servant, for justice in a democracy is serving the people by any and all means. The sausage-seller, by contrast, depicts Paphlagon's political work in apolitical terms. Politics is theft, and Paphlagon is just another thief. The sausage-seller strips the political realm of its special character, thereby depriving Paphlagon of the respect he seeks, and at the same time, suggesting that the lowest knave could do as well or better.

Paphlagon's prayer attempts to make believable his bogus principle of right. Paphlagon needs to enunciate this principle to justify his conduct and Athens' status as a city. Unless right exists, why should Demos continue to hold trials? With his superior strength, Demos, or his hired hand, could just take what he wants. There is no need for trials and assemblies. Without right, the city cannot be justified. And, without right the city need not be justified. Thus, there is no need for Paphlagon. The sausage-seller in depicting Paphlagon as a thief attempts to lay bare Athens' injustice in the hope that Paphlagon will no longer be able to use right in order to enthuse Demos into leaving his home. The Pnyx is nothing holy.

Paphlagon attempts to make politics look attractive to Demos by pronouncing the most demagogic principle of justice one could ever formulate. Justice is whatever is good for Demos. Given the fact that Demos is poor (945), one may say that justice is taking from the rich and giving to Demos, or justice is equality.

In most democracies, the injustice of this principle is partially obscured by the people's number. Many people accept the formulation that, justice = the will of the many. Aristophanes, by making Demos one instead of many, makes Demos' injustice manifestly clear. Paphlagon thinks that by feeding Demos this manifestly unjust principle he solidifies his power. Ironically, however, he undermines it. For by attempting to justify political life by means of masking selfishness as justice, he ripens Demos for the suggestion that Demos' own self-interest is threatened by political life itself.

After bringing Paphlagon down to his level, the sausage-seller challenges Paphlagon's professed love:

> But that he neither loves nor is devoted to you, this very thing first I'll teach you, except merely for the one reason that he enjoys the warmth of your hearth (779-780).

Unlike Paphlagon in his last entreaty to Demos, the sausage-seller does not acknowledge the public. In his last entreaty to Demos (773-6), Paphlagon split Athens into the public and the private, with himself and Demos being in the former, and everyone and everything else being in the latter. By contrast, according to the sausage-seller, everything is Demos' private property, and Paphlagon befriends Demos in order to benefit from it. He is interested in Demos not because of Demos, but because of Demos' hearth. Paphlagon does not love Demos, he loves Demos' things. For Paphlagon, Demos is only a means of satisfying his own needs. Paphlagon is a practitioner of the mercenary love he attempts to foist onto Demos.

After suggesting that Paphlagon loves Demos' things, not Demos, the sausage-seller lets Demos know that he does not make the same mistake. He loves Demos himself:

> You who crossed swords with the Medes at Marathon concerning your land and winning this victory you gave to us powerfully to lash out with our tongue (781-2).

Whereas Paphlagon speaks about his own actions, the sausage-seller speaks about Demos'. Paphlagon wants Demos to regard him as worthy of esteem. The sausage-seller lets Demos know that it is Demos who truly merits esteem. According to Paphlagon, Demos should bestow Paphlagon with the benefit of office, because in doing so, Demos indirectly benefits himself—as chief servant of Athens, Paphlagon provides Demos with material comforts. Paphlagon gets Athens' highest honor, Demos gets a meal. With the sausage-seller, Demos gets both. Demos has earned the right to be honored and fed:

> you roughly sitting there on that hard rock he does not care, whereas I sewing this seat bring this for you. Here, lift up, and then gently sit, in order that you do not chafe what fought at Salamis (783-5).

Demos' ass fought at Salamis, therefore Demos' ass is worthy of esteem, not Paphlagon. Whereas Paphlagon wants Demos to adore him as a living monument to democratic virtue, the sausage-seller wants Demos to hate Paphlagon and politics and adore his own ass. For the sausage-seller does. Paphlagon wants to be loved as a lover of Demos. The sausage-seller demonstrates that he loves Demos. What he offers is as direct and immediate as the comfort Demos' ass will derive from the cushion the sausage-seller brings him. Paphlagon and politics deprive Demos of honor and live off the warmth of Demos' hearth. Paphlagon is a parasite. As long as there is political life, there will be politicians making speeches and winning the honor that Demos rightfully deserves. In Cleonic fashion, the sausage-seller makes a speech deriding speech.[31] He criticizes Paphlagon for exploiting Demos' heroism in his ("lashing out") speeches, which Paphlagon delivers in order to drum up enthusiasm for one thing or another. Speech is the means by which Paphlagon makes political life alluring. In depicting political speech as just one more good stolen from Demos by his servants, the sausage-seller attempts to strip political life once and for all of its seductive costume. The city is land, and the Pnyx is just a rock which causes injury to Demos' holy ass. Politics is painful. Demos has earned the joys of private life.

The sausage-seller's gift works to great effect. Demos is very pleased:

> Human being, who are you? Are you not some descendant of the house of Harmodius? Let me tell you this deed of yours is truly noble and people-friendly (786-787).

By giving Demos a mere cushion, the sausage-seller leads Demos to believe that he is a descendant of the house thought to have founded contemporary Athenian democracy. His good deed has caused Demos to consider him as one of those who gave birth to Demos' regime. The son has become a father, and he will soon give Demos another birth (1319-28). First, however, the sausage-seller must win the battle at hand. Towards this end, the sausage-seller has just taken a big step, for in speaking about Demos' noble past, the sausage-seller has projected a noble appearance—he (the sausage-seller) looks noble in the eyes of Demos. For immediately after the sausage-seller reminds Demos of his noble past, "noble" pops up in Demos' vocabulary. The sausage-seller, by making Demos see himself (Demos) as noble, is himself (the sausage-seller) seen by Demos as noble. But what does Demos see? Like Paphlagon, we are driven to say to Demos, "from such tiny favors you have become well-disposed towards him [the sausage-seller]!" (788).

In answering this question, Paphlagon's incredulousness is a guide to us. Paphlagon is incredulous, because the sausage-seller's move transcends Paphlagon's own understanding of democracy. His model of democracy is to use the city to cater to Demos' appetites. By any and all means, he uses the political realm to produce for Demos economic goods. Since Paphlagon regards the sausage-seller as providing a mere tidbit, Paphlagon cannot understand the response this tidbit generates in Demos. Paphlagon, the political man, now seems only to appreciate the economic.

For this reason, Paphlagon cannot see that the sausage-seller generates this response not with the cushion, but by supplying a poetic account of that for which the cushion is made (890-2). The sausage-seller tells Demos he is noble. Whereas in the Senate it suits the sausage-seller to regard cheap food as dwarfing the importance of the Persian wars, here it suits him to play up the Persian wars in order to make Demos believe in his own nobility. Demos heroically fought and won for Athens her greatest victory. Therefore, Demos deserves comforts, not hardships or trials. Pericles introduces the noble, in order to induce Demos to subordinate the private to the public; Paphlagon eliminates the noble so that nothing will stand in his way in reducing politics to meeting Demos' economic needs; and the sausage-seller reintroduces the noble so as to make Demos believe politics is beneath him. His reintroduction of the noble shows Demos that he has nothing left to prove or do. Rather than mention Athens' current war and the need for Demos to become, once again, heroic and public-spirited, the sausage-seller mentions an old war and Demos' former heroism and public spiritedness, so as to induce Demos to think that Demos has sacrificed enough. Paphlagon makes Demos feel good about his self-interested understanding of political life. The sausage-seller makes Demos feel good about staying home. Paphlagon teaches Demos that the expedient is just. The sausage-seller teaches Demos that the pleasant is noble, or beautiful.

Notes

1. 188-94, 334.

2. Thucydides, 2.65. 8-10.

3. 344-51, 353-5, 715, 719-20.

4. See Neil, *Knights*, 101.

5. For a similar account of this part of the play, see Strauss, *Socrates and Aristophanes*, 94.

6. 615. The sausage-seller's transformation foreshadows his later transformation of Demos from ugly to beautiful.

7. See Leo Strauss, *City and Man* (Chicago: University of Chicago Press, 1964), 192-93.

8. Thucydides, 2.65.7,10-11.

9. 335-42, 353-5, 722-3.

10. 50-2, 63-70, 1111-50, 1192-1205. Cf. Thucydides, 2.65.6-13.

11. See 63-6, 235-9, 299-302, 429-46, 475-9, 624-82, 875-80, 1014-24, 1036-43, 1052-3.

12. Cf. Thucydides, 3.37.3-5: Cleon defends his brutal Mytilene policy by posing as the defender of the laws. He chastises the people for revoking the resolution they had just made with respect to Mytilene on the grounds that this resolution has the status of law. Cleon further argues that altering this resolution weakens democratic government, inasmuch as all governments require citizens to have reverence for the laws. Although in the case of Mytilene, Cleon's arguments fail, Athens' later brutal treatment of Scione reveals that Cleon's "law" survives. Thucydides, 4.120-3; 5.32. I am thankful to Seth Benardete for pointing this out to me.

13. Cf. Leo Strauss, *The City and Man*, 212-14; Thucydides, 2.65.8-11.

14. Thucydides, 2.65.8-9.

15. Ibid., 2.34-46.

16. See Strauss, *City and Man*, 212-13.

17. Compare 411-4 to 415-6.

18. 725-6, 1214-5.

19. Paphlagon may have in mind eligibility to vote. As Aristotle mentions in Book III of his *Politics*, eligibility to vote is everything in a democracy. As Chief Ruler, Paphlagon could make Demos larger simply by increasing the voting allowance or smaller by decreasing it. And since in the play Demos seems to represent the voting public, such action would naturally cause Demos to expand and contract.

20. Although here Aristophanes may not have in mind the story of man's origins that Plato has Aristophanes narrate in the *Symposium*, I refer to it because it illustrates the distinction I believe Aristophanes here is making between Zeus and Paphlagon.

21. Or more literally, "who does you injustice (*adikei*)?"

22. Compare lines 637-38 with 215, 181, and 218.

23. Cf. 391-4

24. See 417-20.

25. With the sausage-seller, the public will vanish in name as well as in reality.

26. *Despoine*, feminine of despot.

27. She reigns over the entire city, and is therefore concerned with the entire city's good, i.e., justice.

28. The sausage-seller's suggestion that he be cut up and boiled with mincemeat parallels Paphlagon's. The sausage-seller offers to subject himself to his own art, as did Paphlagon.

29. Cf. Strauss, *Socrates and Aristophanes*, 92, 94, 102-3 and 107 for his observation of the sausage-seller's filial love for Demos.

30. *Semnon* may also mean holy.

31. Thucydides, 3.38.2-7.

CHAPTER FIVE

The Final Victory of Pleasure

The remainder of the play solidifies the sausage-seller's victory over Paphlagon. After the sausage-seller endears himself to Demos with his gift, Paphlagon strikes back by boasting that he is willing to offer his head if "any man appeared" loving Demos more than he (790). But "any man" has appeared, and therefore Paphlagon is doomed. "Any man" is the sausage-seller, the product of a distinctionless choice, who blurs all distinctions. He has no standards to live up to, and therefore will not impose any on Demos. He epitomizes democracy. Paphlagon does not, because he tries to maintain the distinction between the public and the private. He must maintain the political, in order to remain political leader. However, Paphlagon's reduction of the political to the economic leaves him with no response to the sausage-seller's attack on the political in the name of economics.

The sausage-seller challenges Paphlagon's love by citing the pain Paphlagon imposes on Demos by continuing the war (792-6). Paphlagon's war policy makes Demos' home life harsh. In the Senate, the sausage-seller is pro-war.[1] In the Assembly, pro-peace. In both cases, however, the sausage-seller eyes the same objective: a private good. In order to make Demos endure the hardships of war, Paphlagon tells Demos that his endurance will be rewarded with empire (797-800). Paphlagon will make Demos' regime universal. He will apply his notion of justice around the globe. He tries to make the political realm appealing to Demos, by showing Demos that through politics Demos can have the whole world. In holding out this tempting prize, Paphlagon says nothing about the honor it could bring. Empire is not an opportunity for Athenians to make evident strength of soul. He presents empire not for honor's sake, but for the sake of a meal. With empire, Demos will receive a 2 obol a day pay raise. For Paphlagon, politics is never about man's ability to transcend body. Politics is rooted in the body, and extends the body's range. The city is a leviathan.

The sausage-seller discredits Paphlagon's defense of politics and his imperial designs by arguing that empire will not make Demos happy. Empire may bring jury pay, but money is only an intermediate good. Pleasure is a final good. Paphlagon offers obols, the sausage-seller offers walks in the countryside and meals of oats and pressed olive (805-9).

Paphlagon responds by chastising the sausage-seller for treating him, a man "having done more good by far for the city than Themistocles," without due regard (810-2). Paphlagon compares himself with the great Themistocles, evidently, because he, like Themistocles, makes Athens' presence known and felt in Greece and beyond. That Themistocles accomplished this is clear. In fact, his policies laid the foundation for the imperialism that Paphlagon presently pursues. Themistocles fortified the city, developed the navy, and had the Peiraeus built. These policies enabled Athens to rule the seas. By ruling the seas, Athens could envision herself ruling anywhere. Themistocles gave birth not only to imperial practice but also to the imperial idea: Athens can be anywhere. However, whereas Themistocles induced Athenians to abandon their material possessions for the sake of the city, Paphlagon makes Demos' material possessions the purpose of political life.

So, whereas both Paphlagon and Themistocles, one might say, strive to make Athens powerful, Paphlagon makes Athens dependent on her material appetites, whereas Themistocles tried to free her from them. Moreover, far from surpassing Themistocles' achievements in power politics, Paphlagon undoes them. After Pylos, Athens could have forced Sparta to accept terms, and with her empire intact, could have continued to extract tribute from her allies. Given Athens' and Sparta's contrasting dispositions,[2] with time Athens would have become stronger, and, in relation to Athens, Sparta weaker. In peace, Cleon could have achieved victory for Athens. Instead, Paphlagon allows the war to continue, needlessly exposing Athens to the risk of defeat. And with defeat, Athens eventually loses the influence that Themistocles helped her achieve. Placed in the same situation, it is hard to believe that Themistocles would have made the same mistake. Furthermore, Paphlagon misuses the imperial power that Themistocles did much to create. Paphlagon advocates brutal policies.[3] He wields in barbaric fashion the strength that Themistocles enabled Athens to develop. Paphlagon, "the man from Paphlagonia," would make Athens as barbaric as the land with which his name is associated. Themistocles, unlike Paphlagon, could never be confused with a barbarian. His understanding of affairs made him a citizen of the world. After being forced to flee Athens, he lived out his life as an advisor to the Persian king. If the barbarian is absolutely other, Themistocles is most unbarbaric.

Given Themistocles' effect upon Athens' spirit and power, and his uncanny cosmopolitanism, Paphlagon's comparing himself with him is utterly comic. His assertion must have Themistocles rolling in his grave; the sausage-seller's response to it will have the audience rolling in the aisles. For the sausage-seller fashions a response that induces Demos to associate the sausage-seller, not Paphlagon, with Themistocles (884-6). And though we might have predicted this, having seen the sausage-seller turn the tables on Paphlagon time and again, how he accomplishes this feat is worth noting.

After Paphlagon chastises the sausage-seller for besmirching his Themistoclean service to Athens, the sausage-seller chastises him in return for this unconscionable comparison. The sausage-seller grandiloquently cites Themistocles' accomplishments, strongly suggesting that Paphlagon's do not measure up. And, what accomplishments of Themistocles does the sausage-seller mention? Not his generalship, not his daring diplomacy, not his incredibly important fortification of the city, not his effect upon Athenian public spiritedness. Instead, the sausage-seller cites Themistocles' effect upon the Athenian pantry. He gave Athens a larger and more diverse cuisine (813-9). It is through this clever but skewed reinterpretation of Themistocles' significance, it would seem, that Demos is led to accept the sausage-seller as his "new Themistocles."

The sausage-seller is able to make Demos see all things abstracted from their political significance, to see all things in terms of the private realm. So, Themistocles was great because he made Athens a great food emporium, while Paphlagon is a scoundrel because he makes it small (817-8), because he is a glutton (823-27), and because he will starve Demos if necessary (855-57).[4] The leader who increases Athens' food supply is a hero, the man who eats too much is a traitor. The vexing public policy problem of the day, the Peloponnesian War, does not come up. Under Pericles, Athens is the school of Greece. Under Paphlagon, Athens will become like Sparta: mercenary, brutal, self-righteous and self-ignorant.[5] Under the sausage-seller, Athens would cease to be a city, and Demos would be a barbarian. Life would be reduced to food and sex.

The sausage-seller also makes Paphlagon's inequality work against him. He comes to be seen as undemocratic, so none of his pandering works (868-70, 890-92). By contrast, Demos judges the sausage-seller the best and most devoted man to the city, because he tends to Demos' toes (873-4). Evidently, Demos is satisfied that the sausage-seller is willing to stoop to any low in order to satisfy Demos. Demos has seen enough, and is poised to take his wedding ring away from Paphlagon and give it to the sausage-seller (947-8). Just then Paphlagon beseeches Demos to hear his oracles before finalizing the divorce, and so the contest continues (960-66).

The fight in the Assembly is an elongated version of the fight in the Senate. In both places, Paphlagon goes from justice to the gods to food. First he makes an accusation intended to make his adversary pay the penalty. When it turns out that his juror cares more about himself than justice or the political realm, he brings in the gods in order to sanctify himself and the political realm. When this fails, he tries simple handouts (1151-1258).[6] Paphlagon's efforts are futile, for all the sausage-seller has to do to turn things in his favor is ask Demos to compare Paphlagon's well-stocked "hamper" with his own. Because the sausage-seller's is empty, Demos concludes that it has the democratic spirit (1216). Moments later the sausage-seller is declared Demos' new guardian (1259-60).

In the play's final episode the meaning of the sausage-seller's regime is brought to its logical conclusion. With marvelous ingenuity he restores old man Demos to youth by "boiling him down" (1321), removes from Paphlagon's chambers the peace terms, personified as beautiful women, and presents them to rejuvenated Demos (1316-1408). The sausage-seller not only enables Demos to experience the justice within the city as a private pleasure, he enables him to experience the justice between cities as a private pleasure. The victory of the sausage-seller represents the absolute conquest of the private over the public, a victory that is necessitated by the motion inherent to democracy.

In pleasing Demos, the sausage-seller has become noble in the eyes of Demos. Demos comes to embody one more equation, the noble = the pleasant. If the noble = the pleasant, the noble must disappear, because whatever nobility is, it requires one to subordinate one's pleasure for the sake of something else. This something may turn out to be, in part or in whole, pleasant, but still one has had to wait. Paphlagon tells Demos that Demos will rule "all Greeks . . . if he waits" (797-99). Although becoming universal tyrant may be ignoble, Paphlagon's remark illustrates the power of the noble. It encourages man to develop virtue without which man can never become other than what he is. If the pleasant = the noble, man ceases to be the being who can become. The sausage-seller promises Demos walks in the countryside and meals of oats and pressed olive because under his rule this is all Demos will be able to afford (805-7). Under Paphlagon, Demos aspires to evil, but in leaving Demos with aspirations, he leaves him with virtues without which Demos could never become good.

Although Paphlagon appeals to Demos' moderation (in beseeching Demos to wait in order for his policy to bear fruit), Paphlagon cannot use this in his contest with the sausage-seller. For if Demos comes to appreciate the importance of virtue, Paphlagon would beat the sausage-seller, but lose to everyone else. Instead, he thinks he can beat the sausage-seller by portraying himself as the man who will bestow empire upon Demos. Empire sounds good to Demos (1011-14), however, only because it means being showered with health and wealth (1090-1). Even when Paphlagon expands the political realm as far as it can go, all he offers Demos are private goods. Since the private realm belongs to the sausage-seller, Paphlagon cannot win with this argument.

Paphlagon also attempts to gain the advantage by arguing that his regime will provide Demos a higher standard of living than the sausage-seller's (797-800). Paphlagon's promise of a pay raise goes nowhere, however (821-2). Demos is as blind to the distinction between wealth and poverty as he is to the distinction between the noble and the ignoble.

Paphlagon represents the last gasp of the public realm. His defeat by the sausage-seller, therefore, represents the defeat of the public realm. Since honor seems to require the public realm, the defeat of Paphlagon means the defeat of honor. How does the elimination of honor affect the private realm and the life of consumption that Demos will lead under the sausage-seller? The play suggests that the elimination of honor means that Demos loses the ability to distinguish between a life of high consumption and mere consumption. In contemporary terms, how much does the economic prosperity of "free-market" countries depend on the pursuit of honor and the political realm?

Demos' blindness to the noble is part product of this democratic regime, and part due to the suggestion of the sausage-seller. The sausage-seller takes Demos' regime to an even greater level of equality. Just as Paphlagon redefines justice to suit Demos, the sausage-seller redefines nobility to suit Demos. Paphlagon tells Demos, justice = Demos' self-interest. The sausage-seller tells Demos, nobility = a soft seat for Demos' ass. Under the sausage-seller, being noble does not mean subordinating one's body to a higher cause, being noble means to become absorbed in one's own body. The sausage-seller's definition of the noble prevents Demos from ever being noble. At bare minimum, being noble requires one to draw a distinction between self and other. The sausage-seller teaches Demos that his nobility does not involve recognizing an other, only himself. The other has become an extension of Demos. Demos incorporates everything into himself. This is the end to which absolute equality leads. If all things are equal, nothing is distinct, the world collapses into one. It is a unity much like a sausage.[7]

This also comes out in the sausage-seller's "boiling Demos down" (1321). The verb, "aphepso," which we have translated as "boiling down," is metallurgical. It means to make pure. It seems that in purifying Demos, the sausage-seller eliminates the split in Demos between the public and the private. For after being boiled down, Demos becomes thoroughly private. He leaves the city and returns to the countryside.

In boiling down Demos, the sausage-seller gives birth to the first real democracy. For democracy means the rule of demos—a singular, masculine noun. Therefore, democracy is not truly manifest until the people rule and until the people are one. In purifying Demos, in eliminating his public-private split personality, the sausage-seller makes the people one, and so gives birth to true democracy.

That this is so is more than an accident of language. As long as the people are divided, they cannot be said to rule. For as long as they are divided, some rule others. The majority rules the minority; the people do not rule as one unified body. But in order for the people to become one, in order to get true democracy, everything which divides people, all differences, all heterogeneity must be eliminated. As long as there is heterogeneity within the people, the people will always be split between a ruling majority and a ruled minority. Democracy, therefore requires homogeneity. Accordingly, at the end of the *Knights*, the sausage-seller gives us homogenous man, or mass man—a man boiled down into a homogenous unity. The *Knights* shows us what democracy looks like if it were to live up to its name.

And, as the sausage-seller himself shows, hyper-democracy generates one more equality. Equality taken to an extreme means that the sausage-seller may be both Demos' lover (733-5) and his son (725). The sausage-seller's reign pushes Demos to realize the potential inherent in absolute democracy. Erotic love = fatherly love. Demos becomes incestuous. With erotic love, one is attracted to and longs to unite with a particular beloved as a result of the beloved's beauty. With a father's love for a son, one loves the beloved because the beloved is an extension of oneself. Generation not beauty is its basis. Adherence to the principle of his regime forces Demos to combine erotic love and love of the beloved as an extension of oneself. Beauty disappears as a basis of love. Demos longs to unite, to lose himself in his child because the child is another Demos, not because the child is beautiful. Since beauty on its face violates the democratic principle, the regime must support incest. Furthermore, incest gives Demos one less reason to leave home.

Notes

1. See 625-682, especially 667ff, and chapter 3.

2. See Thucydides' account of the Corinthian ambassador's speech at Sparta and the speeches which follow of the Athenians, the Spartan king, and the Spartan ephor, respectively. 1.68-88.

3. See Thucydides' account of the Mytilene debate. 3.36-40, 50.

4. Earlier Paphlagon had asserted that he is able "to make Demos wide and narrow." To Paphlagon's chagrin, the sausage-seller argues that Paphlagon is partly right. Paphlagon makes Demos small or narrow.

5. During the choral ode of lines 973-996, the chorus informs us that when Cleon was a boy he could learn only the Dorian mode of music, suggesting that Cleon has a Spartan soul. Sparta was Dorian. Interestingly, it is during this ode and only during this ode that Aristophanes drops the Paphlagon pseudonym. Here both Paphlagon's real soul and real name are revealed. Cf. 230-3.

6. The fight for Demos' approval seems to have three stages. First, the battle in love speeches (roughly, 763-874), then the battle in oracles (997-1099), and last the battle over who is the true benefactor to Demos (1151-1227). Cf. Dover, 1972, 91-2. It is also possible that that the last two stages should be considered as part of the first—as part of one protracted love speech.

7. Cf. 211-215, 1395-99.

PART II

On the *Assemblywomen*

Introduction

Needless to say, the account of democracy we get in the *Knights* departs substantially from the democracies of our time. With its thuggish politicking and utterly stupid Demos it even departs from the historical democracy of Athens. The demos of Athens, whatever its flaws, were not as bad as the Demos of the *Knights*. In order to reveal the truth about rule and democratic virtue, Aristophanes composes a lie. The internal logic of rule and virtue within a democracy are allowed to progress without limit until they explode on stage in images that would test the capacities of our best animators. What Aristophanes has to teach us in the *Assemblywomen* also will call for a lie, but a very different sort. Given the shift in the subject from the *Knights* to the *Assemblywomen*, this is not surprising. In the *Assemblywomen*, Aristophanes puts on stage not virtue but law, not rule but equality. And since virtue and rule are the opposite of law and equality, for where human beings are perfectly virtuous there is no need for law, and where there is rule, equality is necessarily imperfect, one should not be surprised that the lie of the *Assemblywomen*, or the image it calls for, will be as different as its underlying subject. In the *Knights*, as Demosthenes says, the question that must be answered is, "who?" (72). In the *Assemblywomen*, the question that must be answered is not who, but "what"? What law will save Athens?

Although the shift in focus that occurs from the *Knights* to the *Assemblywomen* will become apparent as we proceed, it might be well to repeat an earlier observation. In the *Knights*, the question of rule occupies the whole play. In the *Assemblywomen*, the question of rule is decided in the first third of the play, and the new ruler disappears in the play's second half. The *Assemblywomen* makes clear that the depiction of democracy it presents abstracts from the very issue which drives the *Knights*. And, the issues with which it is concerned, law and equality, were themselves suppressed in the *Knights*.

The *Assemblywomen*'s view of democracy is very different from that of the *Knights*. The former suggests that democracy runs the risk of blurring all distinctions, or of taking its founding principle—equality—too seriously. The latter suggests that democracy runs the risk of taking rule too seriously, or of thinking that justice should extend into every aspect of human life. Although Paphlagon induces Demos to accept this view, Demos is ripe for it. And as we mentioned, Paphlagon is only one of the Paphlagonians. There are others who could induce Demos just as well. The sausage-seller overcomes Paphlagon and enables Demos to avert tragedy, but only because he has recourse to magic. Aristophanes suggests that only a god can save democracy. The best proof that the *Knights* has a different purpose from the *Assemblywomen* is the character Demos. The character Demos enables Aristophanes to ignore the very problem which motivates Praxagora's reform program: shaping free and equal individuals into a harmonious whole. The principle of equality does not show up in the *Knights*, because it cannot show up. The *Knights*' central conceit ("Demos") disposes of it before the play even begins.

The *Knights* and the *Assemblywomen* illustrate diametrically opposed models of freedom. In the *Knights*, freedom is achieved for Demos by freeing him from the obligations and conventions of political life. In the *Assemblywomen*, freedom is achieved for the demos by means of the law and its perfection. The dichotomy of the *Knights* and the *Assemblywomen*, roughly speaking, is similar to that of Rousseau's *Reveries* and his *Social Contract*. The former suggests freedom is possible only outside of society. The latter suggests that freedom is possible only when society is made absolutely subordinate to law:

> Thus, in order for the social compact to avoid being an empty formula, it tacitly entails the commitment—which alone can give force to the others—that whoever refuses to obey the general will will be forced to do so by the entire body. This means merely that he will be forced to be free (*Social Contract*, I. vii).

For Praxagora as for Rousseau in the *Social Contract*, far from freedom being in tension with the law, freedom is completely dependent upon the law.

Not only does the *Assemblywomen* warn us against the dangers of taking equality too seriously, it also warns us that a democracy of commercial freedom and political participation is not far removed from a democracy without either commercial freedom or political participation. Some twenty-four centuries before several of our commercial democracies seemed on the path towards mandated equality, Aristophanes' *Assemblywomen* warns about the possibility. Given the parallels between his play and subsequent events, we may say that Aristophanes understood a fundamental truth about democracy. Having seen this much, we have seen a lot; however, if this is all we see, we have not seen enough. For Aristophanes' *Assemblywomen* is more than just a lighthouse to statesmen and concerned citizens sailing in a democratic ship of state. For democracy is more than just a regime, it is a psychology or way of thinking about human life. The *Assemblywomen* provides a representation of this psychology or way of thinking. It depicts not only a political dynamic but also a philosophic dynamic. It addresses human beings and citizens.

We begin to see the *Assemblywomen* in a deeper light when we observe that Praxagora's reform is but a particular case of a law being written down and applied throughout the city. Not only does the *Assemblywomen* teach us not to take equality too seriously. It also teaches us not to take the law too seriously.[1]

Athens is a good setting for Aristophanes' teaching because Athens loves to innovate.[2] And, although Praxagora, as I shall show, must overcome this love, there is a connection between innovation and the law. To innovate is to reject the old, or the tried and true, for the new, or the untried and seemingly true. In order to replace the experientially true with the seemingly true requires faith in reason, in the mind's eye as opposed to the eye of experience. So does a reformer of the law, because law presupposes that a particular generalization will retain its validity into the future. Like innovation, the law-reformer requires faith in reason or in the mind's ability to see what cannot be seen.

Athens is a good setting for a play about the law also because it is a democracy, and democracy and law go together. Democracy likes a government of law, because such a government provides order with the least possible violation of its founding principle—equality. When law governs, or is thought to govern, a democratic citizen is not irritated by those who rule, for rulers are just following orders. A government of law neither stokes the pride of rulers nor wounds the pride of the ruled, for in ruling and obeying both are beholden to the law. That democracy reflexively prefers the rule of the law is supported by a cursory look at the American Founding. A common criticism of the anti-Federalists of the Federalists and their Constitution was that it meant a return to arbitrary, unrepresentative government. In opposing the presidency, the anti-Federalists thought of themselves as being for "a government of laws not men."[3]

By the same logic, proponents of democracy favor writing the law down, so that the people may know what it is, and can be sure that they are being ruled in accordance with the law, not the will of those in charge, or of some dark and necessarily arbitrary "nocturnal council." Writing the law down gives everyone, or just about everyone, access to it. It can be widely known, and therefore it may be widely invoked. The requirement that laws be written down also affects the character of the laws themselves. For it imposes constraints on the laws themselves. A law which is too complex to be expressed in a written form is ruled out from the start. Written laws are therefore doubly democratic: they are conditioned to be simple and are therefore accessible to the simple-minded, and they offer the condition of accessibility.

Of this the *Assemblywomen* is illustrative. In the hag scene, perhaps the most vivid representation of the ugliness of the law ever composed, the first hag points to a copy of the law. In the American Revolution, despite Jefferson's suggestion in the Declaration that the colonists were the true Englishmen, the founders were not in favor of going with the unwritten English Constitution. It was essential that their fundamental law be written down. If the rule of law is to be preferred to the rule of men, because law has the potential to be pure reason, whereas men at any particular point in time are governed by passion or will, then written law is to be preferred to unwritten law, because it is least subject to his passion or will. The rule of the written law demonstrates more faith in reason than the rule of the unwritten law, because it supposes not only that reason may rule without the aid of active intelligence, but also that the reason embodied by the law may extend its reign over man for all time. The written law tempts man into believing not only that reason may solve man's problems, but that it has within its power the ability to solve man's problems once and for all. The *Assemblywomen* is a reflection upon this all too human temptation.[4]

Notes

1. Of course, to say that equality and the law should not be taken too seriously is not to say that they should not be taken seriously or even very seriously.

2. Thucydides, *The History of the Peloponnesian War*. See both the Corinthian ambassador's speech at Sparta (especially 1.70) as well as Pericles' Funeral Oration (especially 2.38-39).

3. "Our countrymen are entitled to an honest and faithful government; to a government of laws and not of men," The Federal Farmer in Herbert Storing, ed., *The Anti-Federalist, An Abridgement* by Murray Dry (Chicago: University of Chicago Press, 1981): 2.8.64. See also 2.8.23, 2.8.44 and 2.8.49. In these latter citations, one does not see the phrase expressed, but the sentiment is there.

4. My treatment of the law and the distinction between law and rule owes much to Book III of Aristotle's *Politics*. Although in Book III Aristotle makes clear that the rule of the law is undesirable, he also makes clear why we might regard it as attractive.

> One might perhaps assert, however, that it is bad for the authoritative element generally to be man instead of law, at any rate if he has the passions that result [from being human] in his soul (1281a34-37).

Aristotle, *Politics*, trans. Carnes Lord (Chicago: University of Chicago Press, 1984). See also 1282b1ff, 1286a8-1286b9, 1287a20ff.

CHAPTER SIX

Praxagora's Lamp[1]

The *Assemblywomen* begins with Praxagora addressing her lamp in the following words:[2]

> Oh bright eye of the lamp spun from a potter's wheel, most beautifully having been discovered in clever minds. For your birth and fortune we shall show. For in circular motion being driven from a rush of potter's earth, your nostrils emit a light worthy of the sun (1-5).

Praxagora does not just praise her lamp. She deems it a god.[3] Her address is in the form of a prayer. In addressing her lamp as a divine being, Praxagora feels compelled to explain herself, as she follows with two explanatory clauses.[4] In the first, Praxagora identifies as the reason for regarding her lamp a god its birth and fortune. And, in the second, she supplies an account of its birth. The account of the lamp's fortune is apparently dropped. She does not demonstrate the luck of the lamp, let alone connect this demonstration with her assessment that the lamp is a god. One might argue that the account of its birth also contains an account of its fortune, as birth seems to have something unpredictable about it. Praxagora has just said, however, that clever minds devised her lamp. It is not born, it is made. It is the product of science, or techne.[5] Luck has nothing to do with it. Why is fortune mentioned as an explanation, and then left unexplained?

In the second explanatory clause, in which Praxagora gives an account of the lamp's birth, Praxagora makes clear that the lamp's divinity is due to its capacity to produce light. As she says, "[its] light is worthy of the sun." Here we note two things. First, given the mechanical necessity with which a lamp produces light, it once again seems that fortune has nothing to do with the divinity of the lamp. Second, in basing the divinity of her lamp on its capacity to produce light, Praxagora reduces the gods to their natural office.[6] She implies that man's technological capacity, or ability to manipulate the natural world, enables him to replace the Olympian and cosmic gods with those of his own making. The ease with which Praxagora elevates a human artifact to the level of Helios signifies her belief that the gods do not enforce or represent transcendent moral principles, for if the gods did represent transcendent moral principles, Praxagora could not regard her lamp as worthy of the honor of the Sun. According to Praxagora, man's inferiority to the gods is one of magnitude not direction. Man does not require the moral direction of the gods. Helios is just a brighter lamp, not a more knowing one.

Under the circumstances Praxagora's demotion of Helios and promotion of her lamp is remarkable. For she is about to lead an army of women into the highly uncertain realm of the Assembly. Therefore, one would expect her to try to endear herself to rather than alienate herself from the gods.[7] Praxagora is a proto early modern. Man is a technological animal, and nature is raw material upon which man with techne may exert absolute control. Across nine of Aristophanes' eleven extant plays, nature (*phusis*) appears thirty-nine times, but in the *Assemblywomen* not once.[8] Praxagora has good reason to hail her lamp and the technology from which it springs, for she too is a maker. Praxagora has in mind to craft a city.

Immediately after deeming her lamp on a par with Helios, Praxagora says:

> Send out the agreed upon signal of flame! (6).

The lamp may be a god, but it is utterly subordinate to human authority, for it may be issued commands. Praxagora then continues praising her lamp, citing it for being useful to the secret schemes of women. It illuminates and guides the hands and other body parts during sex, and it enables women to secretly grab food and wine from the storehouses (7-15). And, as she says, "these things you don't blab to neighbors" (16). The lamp's inferior power of illumination compared with Helios turns out to be its strength. It reveals only what its owner wants shown. Helios, by contrast is a chatterbox. He reveals all things to all indiscriminately. Helios exposes and therefore destroys the private realm, the site of man's most intense pleasures. Praxagora's god, however useful during the night, is useless with the arrival of dawn, for with the sun's arrival there is no longer a private realm left for the lamp to illuminate. Praxagora's invented city, one might argue, will do the lampmakers one better, for it will enable Athenians to enjoy private pleasures in the bright light of day. No longer will citizens need to wait for darkness. No longer will they need their lamps. That citizens will choose to retain their lamps suggests that Praxagora's city is a failure.[9]

In Praxagora's clever mind is a scheme for providing citizens with an equal share of bodily pleasures. In attempting to distribute sexual pleasure equally, she even has an answer for the accident of birth. Her regime represents the technocratic conquest of chance. Fortune drops out by necessity.[10]

Praxagora's attempt to conquer chance is evident in the "rehearsal" scene which immediately follows. Having been drawn by Praxagora's signal flame, her comrades gather around so she can see whether they have followed instructions (57-59). In order to get into the Assembly, the women agreed to dress like men, stop shaving, get tanned, and to don beards (57-77). After inspecting their appearance, Praxagora moves next to what they will say (116-9), and asks for volunteer mock speakers (130). After a first and then a second speaker make mistakes, Praxagora says, "stop . . . as I would not take one more step for the Assembly, unless these things shall be exactly right" (160-2). After the second woman makes yet another mistake, Praxagora orders her to sit, declares that she will speak (163-71), and does giving the longest continuous speech of the play (171-240). Earlier, in response to an objection that the women could not win control of the Assembly due to their lack of experience, Praxagora says, "for this *we* have gathered here, in order that *we* may practice here and know what things it is necessary to say" (115-9, my emphasis). Praxagora, however, ends up absorbing all the practice time herself. Just as with the citizens after she reforms the city, her fellow women are left with little or nothing to do.[11] Her conquest of chance requires that her fellow women forfeit their chance to practice and improve their own speech.

Is Praxagora's city a device for the universal betterment of all, or are others the accidental beneficiaries of a device she designs to please herself? This dilemma, which comes to light here, grows more prominent as the play progresses, as it becomes clearer that Praxagora is the prime beneficiary of the laws she proposes. So, is the *Assemblywomen* really about the law, as we have suggested, or is it a play which once again lampoons the dimwitted Athenian people for falling prey to yet another clever bamboozler?

Notes

1. For an illuminating account of the opening of the play see Bowie, *Aristophanes*, 254-6. Although our accounts differ, I agree that Praxagora's hymn to her lamp "becomes an emblem for the take-over by the world of women of the world of men" (255). Strauss compares the opening soliloquy of the *Assemblywomen* with those of the *Clouds* and *Acharnians*. In all three, the main character (Strepsiades of the *Clouds* and Dikaiopolis of the *Acharnians*) makes known a desire that serves as the plot of the play. Strauss notes an interesting difference. Whereas in the *Clouds* and *Acharnians*, the lead character has help (Socrates and Amphitheos, respectively), Praxagora must rely on her own devices. Thus, Praxagora may be the most extraordinary human being in the entire Aristophanic corpus, more so than Agoracritus, who would have remained anonymous if not for the knights and Demosthenes. Strauss also notes that Praxagora's speech is of singular breadth, foreshadowing the singular breadth of her reform program. Strauss, *Socrates and Aristophanes*, 263-5.

2. The text is doubtful for line 2. For a discussion of alternative readings to this line see Ussher, *Ecclesiazusae*, 71.

3. See Ussher, *Ecclesiazusae*, 70-1.

4. Lines 3 and 4 both begin with an explanatory particle.

5. Just as at the beginning of the play, Praxagora employs a lamp to conquer nature and the sun, at the end, Praxagora employs the law to conquer beauty. Or, as Strauss says, "The triumph of the hags reflects the triumph of Praxagora. It is the triumph of art over nature: Not the sun, but the lamp is Praxagora's emblem" (*Socrates and Aristophanes*, 280).

6. *Helios* in Greek means either the sun or the sun god.

7. The fact that Helios' function was believed to have been taken over by Apollo at some point in the fifth century B.C. only makes this more remarkable. Recall that in the *Knights*, Paphlagon's first words upon entering the Assembly are, "to *despoina* Athena, *ruler* of the city, I pray" (763-4, my emphasis). While Praxagora opens her rehearsal speech with a prayer, it confirms my point. "I pray to the gods that I drove straight the things that were planned." Her concern is not for the future, but for the past. If her plans were driven straight, all is fine. Nothing can go wrong. This is the prayer of someone who has complete faith in her techne.

8. It also fails to appear in the *Acharnians*. By my count it occurs twice in the *Knights*, at 141 and 518. At 141, Demosthenes asserts that Paphlagon's rival will be of a beyond-nature profession. At 518, in the parabasis, the chorus asserts that the audience, that is, the Athenians, has an ephemeral nature.

9. Cf. 730-876. In this scene, which occurs immediately after Praxagora has outlined her communistic city, an un-law-abiding and law-abiding citizen debate each another. Despite the arguments of the law-abiding citizen and Praxagora's laws, the un-law-abiding citizen refuses to relinquish his private possessions, or his self-interest. Since it is likely that a lamp is among the possessions that he refuses to relinquish, one may say that he and others like him will continue benefiting from the use of their lamps.

10. At *Knights*, 61-63, Demosthenes tells us that Paphlagon by making use of oracles reduces rule to a science. Literally, "he makes for himself a *techne*." So, Paphlagon, like Praxagora, attempts to eliminate chance. However, Paphlagon's science is inextricably tied to his person, or so he deludes himself into believing. He thinks only he knows how to wield the science of demagoguery. The sausage-seller shows Paphlagon that if rule is reducible to a science, anyone who understands the science better than he does deserves to rule.

11. Cf. 239-40.

CHAPTER SEVEN

Praxagora's Political Philosophy: A Study of Her Rehearsal Speech

Since the city that will eventually come to be is Praxagora's idea, the speech she gives in rehearsal merits close attention. For though it is a rehearsal speech, it is the only speech Aristophanes permits us to hear. The "actual" speech that Praxagora makes to the Assembly Aristophanes mostly leaves to our imagination.[1] Although later in the play in the presence of her comrades, husband and an associate, Praxagora attempts to make another speech, prefacing it with a demand not to be interrupted, she is frequently interrupted. What begins as a discourse ends up a dialogue.[2] In rehearsal, Praxagora may say exactly what is on her mind; she is not constrained by her audience. So, in trying to understand her thought it is fitting that we look to her rehearsal speech.

Praxagora's speech can be separated into four parts: the city and the Assembly (171-188), the city and foreign affairs (192-203), male selfishness (205-12) and the virtues of women (214-40).[3] Part one begins with a prayer to the gods for success and an assertion that she and her listeners both share the land in common. Part one ends with a reference to a rift that has developed in Athens between those who attend the Assembly for money and those who regard such men as worthy of death. So Praxagora begins with what Athenians have in common, the gods and the land, and ends with what helps drive them apart, the Assembly. Although in regard to this rift, Praxagora does not take sides, it seems that this is one reason that, as she says, "she is vexed and bears heavily all the political matters (*pragmata*) of the city" (174-5). The Assembly is supposed to give direction to the city, and yet it seems to contribute instability. Instead of enabling Athens to act reasonably, instead of being an instrument of cohesion, it is a source of conflict. It is an invention Praxagora seems to lament:

> There was a time when we didn't use Assemblies at all (183-4).

Later in the play, in the parados (300-10), the chorus contrasts the assemblymen of today with those of Myronides' time. While the latter were selfless, the former are selfish:

> For now they seek to grab three obols whenever they do something for the public just like clay-carriers (309-10).

Although the chorus is mistaken about Praxagora's intentions, for Praxagora does not intend to restore the Assembly's moral luster, the chorus in decrying the mercenary Assembly of today is following Praxagora's lead. Having heard Praxagora, they reasonably assume that she has in mind to restore the Assembly to its former idealist self. So, why doesn't she? This is especially puzzling in light of the fact that the Assembly is the seat of democratic power, and she later depicts herself as democracy's champion.[4] To attempt an answer, let us rejoin Praxagora's lament about the Assembly.

During the time when Assemblies were hardly used, as Praxagora continues:

> and you at least believed Agyrrios (*Agurrion*) worthless. But now we use Assemblies, and the one taking silver (*argurion*), praises [*Agurrios*] over much (184-6).

With the love of silver (*argurion*) comes the love of *Agurrios*, the politician who proposed increasing the pay for legislators from one to three obols a day. In parentheses I have transliterated the original Greek words, so as to make clear the similarity between the politician and the thing (Agyrrios and *argurion*) which has made that politician appealing to citizens. If pronunciation was anything like it is today, Agurrion and argurion may have been even more difficult to distinguish in spoken Greek than in written Greek, depending on only the first "r" present in argurion, which is difficult to hear. It is hard to believe this is accidental, but why does Aristophanes create this effect?

Let us return to the beginning of part one of Praxagora's speech. After telling us that she is "vexed and bears heavily" the city's affairs, she tells us why:

> For I see her always using base men for rulers. And if anyone might be useful for one day, he becomes base for ten (176-8).

Praxagora defines good and bad politicians in terms of usefulness (*chrestos*). Good politicians are useful. They serve a function. Bad politicians are base, which is to say, given the definition of a good politician, they are useless. Now, the only politician Praxagora names in part one of her speech is Agyrrios. One may say, therefore, he is representative of the useless politician. And yet Agyrrios, in word and deed, is almost indistinguishable from silver, or money. In Greek another common word for money is *chremata*, the root of which is the same as the root of "chrestos," or useful/good.[5] So, the representative useless politician is represented by the word, silver, which epitomizes usefulness, for with silver one may obtain almost anything one deems useful.

According to us and the chorus, Praxagora portrays Agyrrios in a bad light. Given Praxagora's definition of a good politician, this is strange. If we glance ahead to Praxagora's reform program, this grows stranger still. Agyrrios increases the pay of Assemblymen, which makes it more affordable for the poor to attend the Assembly. Praxagora, in turn, communizes property and distributes all things equally to all, which benefits only the poor, for communism leaves the rich with less than they had before. The spirit of their programs appears the same, so why is Agyrrios base? With this question in mind, we turn to the second part of her speech—foreign affairs.

Praxagora begins her treatment of foreign affairs with mention of the alliance. She says so little about it that it is impossible to know exactly which alliance she means.[6] She says only that it was promoted as essential to the city's survival, but after being instituted was unpopular (193-6). Praxagora totally abstracts from the circumstances which may have contributed to the alliance's appeal, and to its subsequent lack of appeal. Nor does she offer her own view of the alliance.

The circumstances are even less important to her next item:

> It is necessary to launch ships. To the poor it seems good, but it does not seem good to the rich and to the farmers (197-8).

Praxagora's here speaks hypothetically. She begins with an assumption. The fleet must be launched. Presumably, for she does not give the reason, the good of the whole city is at stake. About this policy, the city is divided. The good of the city is one thing, so she suggests, and the good of the citizens is another. Athens is one city, but it is divided into several classes, which makes it difficult for it to act as one city even when it must. Now we begin to understand why Praxagora suggests that Agyrrios is base, or useless, despite his seeming usefulness. A politician is only useful when he works towards the good of the whole. In every other case he is base. Agyrrios may enable the poor to attend the Assembly by increasing their pay, but he caters to their self-interest, not to their interest in the public good. He does nothing to make the city a unity.

Praxagora turns to foreign affairs, because doing so promotes the unity of the city. For within the realm of foreign affairs, states recognize one another as discrete wholes, which speak with one voice. And within states, because of the threat of other nations, citizens are induced to think in terms of the city's good. That this is Praxagora's intention becomes clear as her discourse on foreign affairs continues:

> You are vexed with the Corinthians, and they with you; but now they are good, and now you have become good (to them) (199-200).

Despite what Praxagora says, unless all the Corinthians speak with one voice, Athens was not "vexed with the Corinthians," but rather in all probability Athens was vexed with Corinth. Corinth may be one, but surely Corinthian opinion on Athens is not similarly one. In her next remark, she makes more clear the degree of unity she seeks:

> The Argives are stupid, but Hieronymous is wise (201).

Praxagora contrasts the Argives, a people, with Hieronymous, one man. Her comparison seems strange, unless we realize that for Praxagora the unity of the individual human being is the model towards which she looks in constructing her city.[7]

In the second part of her speech, through her account of foreign affairs, Praxagora makes known what she is after—a perfectly united city. In part three, she addresses the obstacle to this unity—male material self-interest:

> For you (all) are, O people, the causes of these things.[8] For despite being paid from the public treasury,[9] you all look to the private, each the thing he acquires, and the common . . . goes astray (205-8).

Since Athenians have different material interests, they support different policies, and Athens, the common, is left to drift. Praxagora's argument extends the line of thought that underlies the hypothetical example of part two. Unite the material interests of citizens, and you will unite citizens. Glancing ahead, in response to the question, "What sort of life will you make?" (673), Praxagora responds:

> Common for all. For I propose to make the city (*astu*) one house smashing all things into one[10] (673-4).

Having reduced political conflict to economic conflict, she supposes that the elimination of the latter will bring about the elimination of the former. Praxagora has in mind to make a whole of the city, which as it stands is divided into parts, and is therefore not really one city at all. It is a given that citizens have separate bodies and are born into different families, which causes the city to be disunited. One might say that Praxagora aims to use the law to overcome our natural separateness, to end divisions, and to make the city truly a city.

In order to understand the implications of Praxagora's solution, however, it is necessary to pay close attention to her speech. For although she concludes that economic divisions must come to an end, in her speech it is clear that not all divisions are economic. First, in a remark previously cited, Praxagora reported a division in the city between those who supported Agyrrios and those who regarded mercenary assemblymen as worthy of death.[11] This division seems moral, not economic. Second, earlier in speaking of the city's external affairs, Praxagora says:

> Peace reared its head, but Thrasyboulos is angry because he himself is not called (202-3).

Evidently, Thrasyboulos, an advocate of peace, was not around to bring peace to fruition when the opportunity for peace presented itself, because he was not recognized as the author of the peace plan.[12] Although Thrasyboulos may be selfish, his motivation does not seem purely economic. He does not crave money but honor.[13] Moreover, he is angry at not receiving it. Does Praxagora's economic explanation explain Thrasyboulos' anger? What is the significance of anger?

Just as Praxagora's understanding of the problem is economic, so is her understanding of the solution. The women must be put in charge, for women are the best economists:

> For I say it is necessary to hand the city over to the women. For in fact we use them for stewards and treasurers in our houses (211-2).

Since the city is to become an economic entity, Praxagora recommends that it be put into the hands of women, for the women can be trusted to use and distribute the city's resources. But what does her solution force the city to give up? The answer to this question is suggested above. When Praxagora says she will make the city one (673-4) she uses "*astu*" not *polis*. In becoming one, ironically Athens will cease to be a city.

In the fourth part of her speech Praxagora delves more deeply into the virtues of women, "And how they are better in their ways than us I shall show" (214-5). Praxagora will supply a proof of female superiority, the first article of which is:

> For first of all they dye their wool with heat according to the old law, every single one of them, and you would not see them introducing novelties (215-8).

After ridiculing male selfishness and praising women for being good with money, Praxagora now takes an unexpected turn, for out of the blue she praises women for their adherence to the "old law." Praxagora's remark is striking. First, as support for her claim that women embrace the old law and shun novelty, Praxagora refers to the sight of men, "you [men] would not *see* them [the women] introducing novelties" (my emphasis). The sight of men is weak, however, and she knows it. Her plan is predicated on this very weakness. In short, Praxagora's proof is suspicious. Second, Praxagora's claim about women is universal. It is true of all women. In making her case, she never gives particular examples of women. She treats women as a class, and regards the city as governable only by this class. This brings to mind something which should have struck our attention. Praxagora asserts that it is necessary for the city to be turned over to the women, but not to any particular woman. Praxagora tempts us to believe that she has solved the political problem. For the rule of the assemblywomen is government without hierarchy.

In contrast to the women:

> The polis of the Athenians, if it had something good, would not be for being saved, unless she was meddling in something new[14] (218-220).

Praxagora juxtaposes women's adherence to the old law against the city's love of novelty. Why? Why does she risk alienating her audience by attacking their love of novelty? Earlier Praxagora ordered two women to step aside for saying the wrong thing.[15] Is it not now wrong for her to speak in favor of the old law, for the old law was less democratic? Furthermore, is it not strange for Praxagora to disparage novelty while making an extremely novel proposal—that the women be put in charge of the city? Why does Praxagora now frame the distinction between men and women in terms of the old and the new, for doing so opens a can of worms?

Far from acknowledging the newness of her proposal, Praxagora continues to emphasize its conservativism. Women eschew novelty in many ways:

(1) They roast while sitting as they always have.
(2) They carry things on their head as they always have.
(3) They lead the Thesmophoria as they always have.
(4) They bake their flat-cakes as they always have.
(5) They irritate their husbands as they always have.
(6) They have lovers inside as they always have.
(7) They keep dainty dishes for themselves as they always have.
(8) They love wine straight up as they always have.
(9) They enjoy being laid as they always have (221-8).

In order to stress female conservativism, Praxagora employs a constant refrain.

The constancy of Praxagora's words reflects the constancy of women's ways. While her proposal is inarguably new, its novelty is just a cover. It is an old idea in novel dress, or so Praxagora wants her imagined audience to believe. Still, what benefit does Praxagora expect from obscuring the novelty of her proposal while highlighting its oldness?

The phenomenon of Athens' love of novelty Aristophanes constantly draws to our attention. The love of novelty is observed by several characters in the play. Blepyrus, Praxagora's husband, having just heard a report from his friend Chremes about the bold proposition offered at the Assembly, asks, "what was the decision of the meeting?" To which Chremes responds:

> [It was decided] to turn over the city to them [the women]. For it seemed that this was the only thing not yet done in the city (455-7).

And, once again, in the advice the chorus gives Praxagora, as she is about to provide an account of her city:

> Only go straight to the end neither having done nor having said something ever done before. For they (the audience/her interlocutors) hate it if they often view the old things (578-80).

And, once again, in the encouragement Blepyrus gives Praxagora right after she admits fearing that her auditors will be offended by the novelty of her plan (583-5):

> On the contrary, have no fear of innovations. For we do this in preference to anything old. Concerning the old things, we care not (586-7).

The Athenian love of novelty also shows up, in a less direct way, in the two episodes towards the end of the play.[16] In the first, one citizen tries to persuade another not to obey the city's new laws on the grounds that the new laws will eventually go the way of the laws they replaced. Why relinquish your property in observance of laws that will soon be changed? This scene makes explicit the conflict between the law and the Athenian love of novelty. Thus, it does not appear accidental that Praxagora juxtaposes the city's love of novelty against the women's adherence to the *old* law (my emphasis). Praxagora's account of the female adherence to the old law is her noble lie. In order for her laws to fend off the Athenian love of novelty, she gives to the law the stature that time bestows.[17] Her laws are not mere decrees.[18] They are sown in the womb of time, and are delivered into the world by midwife Praxagora. She is not their creator; she merely assists in bringing them to life, that is, delivering them into the public domain.

In the second episode,[19] three hags invigorated and empowered by the law lay claim to the sexual favors of a young man. Praxagora decrees that no lover may have sex with a beloved until he or she gives sex to the ugliest who demands it. All of the hags cite this law.[20] Still, the young man refuses to obey. He makes known his attraction to his girlfriend, who in turn portrays herself as embodying the voluptuousness of youth. So, once again, we see that Athenian men embrace the new and shun the old. Praxagora has made the law venerable, but she has also made it ugly and sterile. What does this mean? And why does the play stress the Athenian love of novelty? What is behind the love of novelty?

As Praxagora has stressed in her speech, Athens is a democracy.[21] That is, in Athens, the people rule. If the people rule, whom do they rule? Answer: the people. The people rule the people. Which is to say that the people establish their own rules, they may live any way they choose. The people have the right of freedom.[22] The possession of power results in the formulation of a right, which reflects the people's awareness of their own power, and provides it with content. Without it the people would not be sure of their power, or what to do with it. What is true of power is true of freedom. The occasion of freedom results in the formulation of a demand or the performance of an action. For without this the people would be left merely contemplating their freedom, or experiencing their freedom through contemplation. The presumption behind the people's seizure of power, however, is that the thought is not enough.[23] To realize freedom, the demos must revolt, and once in power, they must continue to revolt, to certify they remain free. Without the awareness of freedom there is no freedom. Revolting against the past, i.e., the love of novelty, is the logical conclusion towards which democracy leads. For only by replacing the past can the people be sure they are not determined by it. Democracy means orange hair. It means innovation. What is the significance of Praxagora's attempt to uproot so fundamental a feature of democracy?

Democracy's pursuit of freedom results in innovation, because democracy does not just want freedom, it wants to be recognized as free. The people want recognition for their freedom, therefore they innovate. That Praxagora targets the Assembly now makes sense. For not only is the Assembly the origin of Athens' innovations. It is also the site of Athens' self-recognition. And Praxagora knows that if she is to eliminate the one, she must eliminate the other.

What is true of democracy is also true of individual human beings. For human beings freedom and recognizing ourselves as free are inseparable. Therefore, we too experience the same tension experienced by Athens. We want to be the authors of our own actions. Taken to an extreme, this would mean simultaneously reflecting upon our position and re-authorizing it at every moment. Moreover, to certify that our position is our own we would have to remove ourselves from every position imposed upon us, everything related to our birth and childhood. In other words, to certify that we are free requires us to make our own mark. Freedom requires innovation, but innovation compels us to deny the significance of our past, and makes it difficult to think of our lives as forming a coherent whole. Indeed, preserving our freedom, or authenticity, requires that we free ourselves even from our own past innovations, for to the extent they exert an influence we are not free. Our push for freedom pushes us to regard our prior experience as absolutely other. You might say, in order for me really to be me today, I must regard the me of yesterday as someone else. Unless I do, how do I know the experience of yesterday is not constraining my freedom in some way? The drive for absolute freedom results in a multitude of "me"s which are difficult to put together. Knowing ourselves, or making a whole of our past experience, would seem to be as difficult as knowing Heraclitus' river. To understand what the cost would be of perfect wholeness, as opposed to perfect freedom, we must return to Praxagora's perfectly united city.

As a reading of Praxagora's catalogue of female practices suggests,[24] Praxagora uses women as more than just adherents of the old law. One must reflect upon the specific actions that women perform to which Aristophanes attaches the refrain, "as they always have." As I shall show, these actions are not just filling space. Nor does Aristophanes choose them arbitrarily. Praxagora uses women as a class to exemplify the possibility and desirability of a technocratic society.

In practices (1), (2) and (4), Praxagora mentions the staple domestic chores women perform for the benefit of the home: (1), roasting while sitting; (2), carrying things on their head; (4), baking flat-cakes. In (2), Praxagora mentions the evidently old habit women employ of carrying things on their head. But why would women carry things on their head? Women manage the home. Since the home is not self-sufficient, things must be brought in from outside, even from far away, so women have to develop a technique. Moreover, it is not enough for women just to bring things in. Meat must be roasted and bread baked. Nature only provides raw materials; an art is required to make them edible. And, women wield the domestic arts. In (1), (2) and (4), Praxagora presents women as laborers, whose labors entail using an art, and whose labors are lightened by artfulness. Women roast while sitting, and employ their heads as carts. Women use their heads, the means by which human beings ascend to the good, as a tool—which by definition needs to have its good assigned to it. And, as anyone who has carried a heavy object on his head knows, while the head is being used in the second way, i.e., as a tool, it is difficult to use in the first, i.e., as an illuminator of the good. While we are absorbed in the performance of a function, we are not reflecting on the goodness of the function we perform.[25] A person carrying a jug of wine on his head most likely knows where he is going, but does not dwell on whether he should go there. Arts have their goods supplied from outside. And, so must citizens of the artful society.[26] Practice (2) represents more than the moral neutrality of the arts. It represents the necessity of their moral neutrality.

What about (3)—women lead the Thesmophoria? At first, one is struck that Praxagora does not mention (3) first. One would expect Praxagora to give prominence to women's leadership of a religious festival. For it exemplifies their adherence to the old law, while revealing that women are cognizant of the whole. Women think about the city, for their leadership of the festival is a public act. They lead the Thesmophoria for the city's good. Despite (3)'s seeming importance, it is treated as just another item on Praxagora's list. Not only is it not put at the top, it does not change the tenor of the examples that follow. In (4), women are again depicted in a lowly domestic task. Given the nature of Praxagora's other examples, it is surprising Praxagora mentions (3) at all. It sticks out like a sore thumb.

The Thesmophoria was a religious festival in honor of Demeter—the goddess of agriculture, who was called Demeter Thesmophoros, or law-bearing Demeter.[27] Demeter is the goddess associated with a techne, and the law she bears, it would seem, is that which makes up her art. Agriculture represents the ambiguity of the arts. Without agriculture man cannot live, with it man sins. Agriculture requires man to penetrate the Earth's surface, to reach into Hades.[28] Demeter is necessary to sanction this necessary violation. She relieves man's guilt. And, she reminds man that while his reshaping of the Earth is god-like, he is not a god. Arts make man powerful, but they do not necessarily make man good. And the power they impart to man may cause him to forget this fact. You can say that the ambiguity of the art of agriculture is reflected in the need to attach it to a god. And yet, as the festival's name reveals, the god's association with the art is not guaranteed. Who needs the "law-bearing" god, when one has mastered her laws? The Thesmophoria could be just a holiday in honor of farmers. Thus, Demeter is Praxagora's model. She civilizes man, and then she disappears. She is concerned with man's staying alive, not with his lofty aspirations. She is inextricably linked to the Earth.

If this is right, Praxagora's placement of this example makes sense. It is not given a prominent position, because it is not of a higher order than the other examples we looked at. In leading the Thesmophoria, women recognize the important task of working the soil. In (1), (2) and (4), women are shown acting artfully; in (3), paying homage to an art while seeming to pay homage to a god.

The second half of Praxagora's list shows a different side of woman's life. (1) to (4) deal with women's work, (6) to (9) women's pleasures: (6), lovers; (7), dainty dishes; (8), undiluted wine; (9), getting laid. (5), irritating their husbands, is the pivot point. Women's pleasures are the result of their ability to turn the tables on their stronger husbands. Through art they overcome their natural inferiority in physical strength. Thus, in a sense, (6) to (9) are extensions of (1) to (4), for they show women at their most artful. Their manipulative power is so great that even when the object of another's use, they may still experience pleasure.

That Praxagora's catalogue of women's ancient customs ignores the ancient custom of bearing, delivering and raising children is at first shocking. For what could be more ancient or fundamental to women than this, or more worth mentioning? Are not the women petitioning to become mothers of the city? It seems to belong, not only because it exemplifies the ancient character of women's ways but also their technocratic proficiency. Praxagora's omission of women's role as mothers is but one example of the play's almost complete abstraction from this aspect of womanhood.[29] Although why the play abstracts from motherhood and the natural family is not yet clear, an explanation can be offered. Childhood and/or family represents the limit of human artifice. Our birth and childhood calls to mind that we are generated, and imposes a limit upon our ability to make ourselves. Praxagora has in mind to re-make man, so she suppresses this aspect of womanhood.

As Praxagora's presentation makes clear, women are most unlike Athens. Women are practical. All their concerns are for food and sex. Their feet are firmly planted on the ground. The city of Athens, however, is irresponsibly bold. It gives a higher rank to the novel than to its own survival.[30] So, Athenian men are not mere selfish materialists, which is how Praxagora had depicted them. For they care more about living in a certain way—i.e., in a novel way—than living simply. Although pursuing novelty for novelty sake is akin to basing policy upon the lot, and is therefore problematic, the city's love of novelty reveals its ability to transcend the needs of the body. A city governed by women, as Praxagora suggests, would be completely dedicated to the needs of the body.[31] Although a fuller understanding of what this means will come later, Praxagora's closing remarks are suggestive.

In closing, Praxagora says:

> Thusly, if you all should be persuaded by me, you will spend your life being happy (239-40).

The verb which we have translated, "should be persuaded," is the passive of the verb, *peitho*. In the active tense, the verb means to persuade, in the passive, it may mean to be persuaded or to obey. Although the translation above seems right, the alternative is revealing. The men will be happy if they "obey." That is, if they relinquish rule, or submit to having the good supplied to them, instead of formulating the good themselves. If they rest content with benefiting from order, instead of determining the purpose order serves. Praxagora implies that the city can do without the male, i.e., without Assembly speeches debating how to live and what to do. "For," as Praxagora says, "you all consider only this":

> That being mothers first [the women] will desire to save the soldiers. And then who would better send rations than someone who has given birth? (232-5).

Praxagora is saying that the city does not need the Assembly to formulate principles of justice. Communal life does not require self-consciousness. Praxagora has discovered that nature can be harnessed to generate all the fellow feeling necessary to keep citizens from eating one another. The experience of childbirth makes women care. It makes them trustworthy and good.

Notes

1. Chremes offers excerpts from Praxagora's speech, and the Assembly's response to it. See 427-54.

2. See 569-729. At 569-70, Praxagora announces that she will offer a demonstration. At 588-9, Praxagora asks not to be interrupted. At 595, Blepyrus interrupts, and is promptly ridiculed by Praxagora for doing so. A dialogue of sorts ensues.

3. This division is punctuated by exhortations from her troops at 189, 204 and 213.

4. In particular, see 452-3ff, and 630ff.

5. *Chremata* appears at 206, 236, 712, 772, 871 and 873. Moreover, the name of one of the two identifiable male characters is Chremes.

6. Ussher claims the "Anti-Spartan League" of 395 is meant. See Ussher, *Ecclesiazusae*, 102.

7. See Plato's *Republic*, 462c-e.

8. Praxagora employs the plural pronoun and the second person plural form of the verb "to be," followed by the vocative singular of the noun "people." In this sentence, she turns a plural into a singular: all people are collapsed into the singular noun demos. Her intention to collapse all the people into one manifests itself in her rhetoric, just after she forces the people to become one in deed through her discussion of foreign affairs. The end towards which she aims, making the people one, is taken as a given in the *Knights*.

9. In Greek, the people's *chremata*.

10. The Greek word which has been translated "house" has its root in the verb, *oikeo*, from which English derives the word, economics.

11. See 194, above.

12. Thrasyboulos is also mentioned at 356.

13. Thrasyboulos' name means "bold counsel." His name suggests that he is assertive. He defies anonymity, and since Praxagora's pursuit of unity can be accomplished only if individual citizens forego the desire for distinction, there does not seem to be a place for him in Praxagora's city. Therefore, as his name and his actions suggest, Thrasyboulos and those like him will resist Praxagora's city. This points to another distinction between the *Assemblywomen* and the *Knights*. Whereas the *Assemblywomen* suppresses honor in an effort to unify the city, the *Knights* moves toward a situation in which all honor passes through to Demos. At the end of the *Knights*, Demos is dressed in royal attire, whereas the knights and the praise they bestow upon Demos go unnoticed. Only Demos is worthy of esteem. It cannot be an accident that immediately following Demos' entrance he leaves the city for the countryside. If only Demos is worthy of honor, the polis is unsustainable. If Demos does not want to look up to anyone he must be content with the joys of private life. The people have two choices: either being served within political life, and therefore recognizing it rules only indirectly and that those who rule directly are entitled to honor; or, serving themselves in private life.

14. Later in the play, Praxagora will speak before the Assembly during a session dedicated to saving the city. Praxagora will suggest that the women be put in charge. So,

she meets the "the polis of the Athenians'" demand: she "saves" the city while giving it something new (394-7).

15. See 130-143 and 151-160.

16. 730-876, especially 756-68 and 797-822.

17. See, Chremes' remark at 455-7, quoted above. Praxagora's new city comes to be, in part, because of Athens' love of innovation. Unless she eliminates this love, her new city will be undone by it.

18. The Greek word, *psyphisma*, which means decree, is revealing. It is derived from the word for pebble. To count votes pebbles were deposited in an urn. A decree's lack of weight is suggested by the means used to establish it. This word appears here at 813, 816 (as a verb); in the hag scene at 1013, and 1090, and in the dialogue between Praxagora and her two interlocuters, at 649 and 706 (as a verb). Interestingly, while the youngest of the three hags employs "decree," the two older hags employ *nomos*.

19. 877-1111.

20. See 1011-20. The first hag points to the law as she tells the youth that the law compels him. Note that at 1012 she uses a demonstrative adjective with a deictic iota suffix—which has the effect in Greek of pointing to something. The hag then reads the youth the law. Although the other two hags do not seem to be in possession of the law, they both refer to it (1049, 1077, 1078). Said makes the same observation. Said, "Assemblywomen," 310.

21. As she says, "you, O people, are the causes of these things." The people are to blame because the people rule.

22. Cf. 941.

23. This is to say that pure self-recognition is not enough. Demos wants its self-recognition to have a concrete manifestation.

24. See 204, above.

25. Cf. William Shakespeare, *Hamlet*. "Conscience [i.e., reflection or awareness] doth make cowards of us all." I would like to thank Mary Nichols for this reference.

26. This, I think, helps explain why in Socrates' "healthy city" there are no kings, philosophers or philosopher-kings. Socrates' healthy city is another version of the technocratic city, and if any one of the three were present this would reveal that the city was not perfectly technocratic. For a part of the city would not be subject to a techne.

27. Praxagora's entire plan was hatched at the Skira, a festival in honor of Demeter celebrated by women, as Praxagora herself makes known in the soliloquy which opens the play (18). R.G. Ussher calls the Skira an "obscure women's celebration." Ussher, *Ecclesiazusae*, 74.

28. See Sophocles, *Antigone*, 332-375.

29. The play does not completely abstract from women's role as mothers. At 232-5, Praxagora in her rehearsal speech mentions that women being mothers will show more concern for the soldiers. At 527-551, the subject of child-rearing leads Praxagora to announce that children will be raised in common. In the hag scene at 911-918, the young girl discloses that her mother has left her alone in the house. And, at 1038-42, the young girl accuses the first hag of helping to make Athens a city of rampant incest.

30. See 218-20, or pp. 82-83, above.

31. While the democracy of the *Knights* yields a similar result, its meaning in the *Knights* and the *Assemblywomen* is different. That political life gets reduced to the body or to pleasure in the *Knights* signifies that Demos has taken over the city. Only the people are

worth looking up to. In the *Assemblywomen*, political life gets reduced to the body, in part, as we will see, because complete equality requires that we recognize only bodily needs, and that bodily needs be equally met. And, in part, because the absolute rule of the law requires the homogenization of man, which in turn requires that human beings be reduced to body.

CHAPTER EIGHT

The Price of Unity

While Praxagora and her female comrades are in the Assembly, Aristophanes turns our attention to her husband Blepyrus. As she wins control of the city, he sits constipated in her clothing on a city street, barely obscured by the waning night. Because she is in his clothes, he is forced to wear hers. Praxagora's scheme requires women to dress as men, and men to dress as women. After emerging victorious from the Assembly, the women shed their male dress,[1] but Blepyrus remains in his wife's clothing. And while Aristophanes makes clear that the women go back to dressing as women, he gives us no such assurance with respect to Blepyrus. Praxagora's new city requires the suppression of the male.[2]

After having successfully executed her plan, and met with her comrades (478-519), Praxagora returns home to her husband, who tells her what she already knows, that the Assembly has decided to put the women in charge (553-5). In response, Praxagora declares, "By Aphrodite, the city will be happy from now on" (558-9). During rehearsal she reprimanded a comrade for making the very same oath (189), because such an oath would have sounded peculiar in the Assembly, and might have blown their cover. Now that the women are in charge, there is no need for disguise. The women can swear to Aphrodite. Praxagora can make public her model, and force the city to adopt it.

Praxagora says the city will be happy from now on because "being a paid witness (*marturein*) will be nowhere" (561) and (among other things) there will be "no theft," "no envy," "no poor," "no abuse" and "no harrying debtors" (565-7). An anonymous interlocutor,[3] who has just emerged, approves of Praxagora's new city, as long as, as he says, "she does not lie" (568). To which Praxagora responds:

> But I'll prove it. Such that you will be a witness (*marturein*) for me, and this man [Blepyrus] will say nothing against me (569-70).

Aroused by Praxagora's boast and the drama which is about to unfold, the chorus comes forward and urges her

> To arouse sharp thought and a knowing philosophical mind. . . . For . . . the inventiveness of your tongue to our common prosperity is going to gladden the citizen people with countless benefits for life. Now it is time to show what you can do. For the city of ours truly needs some wise contrivance (571-77).

The chorus assumes that the arousal of philosophy and the discovery of a wise contrivance are necessary in order for Praxagora to provide a satisfactory proof, or that "she does not lie." Praxagora's proof will be in the form of a speech, however. It is "of the tongue," not of the hand. For there are no cities like hers to which she can point. So how can her proof not constitute a lie? It does not constitute a lie if and only if human life can be perfectly translated into speech. Theory must perfectly represent practice. The only way that theory can perfectly represent practice, paradoxically, is if practice is devoid of theory. That is, if the city as it proceeds never engages in what Praxagora is about to engage in, a speech setting forth the structure of the city. If in practice the city engages in such a speech, if it has "philosophy," it may arrive at a different understanding of political life from Praxagora's, which would follow in a new regime. For philosophy calls into question all first principles, including Praxagora's. Could Praxagora's regime withstand this questioning? The chorus', albeit flippant, reference to "philosophy" and "wisdom" alerts us to philosophy's absence from Praxagora's new Athens.

A moment earlier Praxagora had boasted that the city will be happy in part because it will have no paid witnesses. *Marturein* will be nowhere. A few lines later, when Praxagora said she would prove that the city she founds would be happy, she asserted that "you will bear witness (*marturein*) for me." Praxagora's use of the same word is suggestive. Being a witness may mean standing guard over a speech. One may stand guard over a speech in a courtroom, or one may stand guard over a speech in a discussion on political life. For Praxagora's regime to sustain itself, it seems both "will be nowhere."

Through the chorus' reference to philosophy and wisdom we gain insight into the significance of Praxagora's name. Praxagora's name combines two words: *praxis*, a feminine noun which may mean practice; and, *agora*, which may denote a public place where speeches are held.[4] As her name suggests, Praxagora combines speech and practice. Her speech, that is her law, strives to remake Athenian practice, or to completely change the way Athenians live. One might say that her law is absolutely practical, not only because it completely changes Athenian practice, but also because it supposes that no future changes will be necessary. For

Praxagora ordains that the Assembly and its furniture should be turned into a huge dining hall.[5] So, not only is Praxagora's speech practical, she gives rise to practice that is meant to replace speech. The implication is that a political life absolutely dedicated to the practical, or the needs of the body, requires the suppression of speech. But why does Praxagora's new city require the suppression of speech? And what does this suggest about the goodness of practicality, if the utterly practical city has no room for speech?

Either philosophy and the intellectual life more generally cannot exist in Praxagora's city, or it must be accorded no honor. For she claims that her city will be devoid of envy and the wise tend to arouse envy, especially when being wise is regarded as a point of distinction. Therefore, Praxagora must keep herself and her technocratic string-pulling obscure lest she become an object of envy. It is no accident that Aristophanes entitled his play *Assemblywomen* and not *Praxagora*.[6] After Praxagora convinces her two interlocutors—Blepyrus and his neighbor, she is not heard from again. Praxagora must figure out a way to make the city technocratic without giving rise to aspirations for honor among the technocratically excellent. For if some are recognized above others, the city will become divided again. If no envy, then no recognition; and if no recognition, no envy.

This comes out in the very beginning of her proof. At 594, Praxagora summarizes the form of her city:

> I am making one common living for all and this living [I make] the same (594).

At this point, Blepyrus interrupts with a question. Praxagora responds with an insult. She is angry because at the outset she demanded that no one interrupt until her proof was finished.[7] She may be making the living common, but she does not want the common speech of dialogue. In angering Praxagora, Blepyrus induces Praxagora to restate the form of her city more precisely:

> First of all I shall make the land common for all and silver and whatever each man has. Then we shall feed you all from the things being in common (597-9).

Praxagora's restatement makes clear not only that citizens will have the same portions but their portions will originate from the same source. Everyone will have the same, and everyone will obtain his livelihood from the same. So no one will feel pride as a result of having more, or doing more.

Not satisfied, one of her interlocutors wants to know about money, "immanifest wealth" (602), or wealth that is hidden from view, and therefore difficult to detect. Praxagora asserts that this too must be handed in, and not doing so makes one a perjurer. Blepyrus cogently responds that "through perjury a person acquires wealth" (603). In other words, Praxagora's program depends on honesty, and it is lack of honesty that enables the wealthy to acquire wealth in the first place. Praxagora needs virtue, but does nothing to instill it, therefore her city will fail. As Praxagora reveals, however, her city has no need of virtue:

> But you know [perjury] will be no use to him at all[8] (604).

Praxagora proceeds to explain that since everyone will have what he needs, perjury or money for that matter will no longer be necessary (605-6). "So what is the profit in not laying things down?" Praxagora defeats the problem of selfishness with selfishness. She conquers the profit motive with the motive to profit, for in laying things down citizens will get a state-provided meal, and if they do not they will go hungry (665-6). Praxagora uses a vice, greed, to sterilize the city from the effects of this vice, inequality. Inequality leads to pride and envy, and disunites the city. To eliminate inequality, Praxagora must rely on vice, for if she depended on virtue she would leave in place another source of pride and envy. Wealth is not the only thing human beings value which is invisible or immanifest. Praxagora's law deals with vice in a very practical way. Rather than reform it, she uses it.

Blepyrus remains unconvinced however.[9] "But even now they steal more, so why not later?"(608). Praxagora repeats almost word for word her remark of a moment ago, "What is the profit of not laying things down?" (610). Blepyrus replies that wealth still will be coveted because with wealth one can win the love of a beloved (611-3). Praxagora responds that "It will be possible for him to sleep with her for free" (613). Praxagora proceeds to give an account of her sex laws, which mandate that the beautiful sleep with the ugly before sleeping with a beloved (614-34). Praxagora's regime equally distributes sex as well as food.

Since no one will need to steal wealth because sex is free, Praxagora eliminates an incentive to steal, as well as a reason for self-restraint. Praxagora's re-designed city renders virtue obsolete.[10] Not only is it not necessary, it is not desirable.

But, one may ask, what about the virtue of law-abidingness? One might argue that Praxagora, at least, promotes this virtue. For if Praxagora's regime works, citizens will have no reason not to obey the law. Obeying the law will be manifestly reasonable, so all will obey the law.

In a scene that occurs immediately following this one, Aristophanes seems to address the present question. Immediately after the above dialogue concludes, Aristophanes presents a scene in which a law-abiding and un-law-abiding citizen debate one another.[11] Although the scene is worth studying in its entirety, I shall limit myself to the following excerpt:

> L.C.: But, why? Isn't it necessary for me to obey the laws?

U-L.C.: Which, O wretch?
L.C.: The ones just passed.
U-L.C.: The ones just passed? You're nuts.
L.C.: Nuts?
U-L.C.: For what else can you be? And the most foolish of all to boot.
L.C.: Because I do what has been ordered (*tattomenon*)?
U-L.C.: For is it necessary for the temperate (*sophrona*) man to do what he is ordered?
L.C.: Most especially of all.
U-L.C.: On the contrary, but the stupid man (762-8).

According to the un-law-abiding citizen, virtue is a substitute for law-abidingness. The virtuous man does not need the law as a guide. His guide is within himself. Only empty men are law-abiding. According to the law-abiding citizen, the virtuous man, especially the temperate man, is law-abiding. For what is temperance but the ability to live within constraints? Together they represent the two objectives of political life: to make citizens better, and to enable them to live together. Law-abidingness is necessary to enable citizens to live together. It promotes order. Whether it makes men better is not so clear. For the perfectly law-abiding citizen is one to whom the possibility of breaking the law would never occur. He is indistinguishable from a slave. Praxagora's regime is ordered, but at what cost? Without order political life is impossible; with nothing but order, the potential of political life goes unrealized.[12]

To appreciate the significance of Praxagora's attempt to eliminate virtue, it might be helpful to reflect upon what virtue represents. As anyone who has read Plato's aporetic dialogues knows, virtue is difficult to define. However, the reason we seek it is perhaps more clear. Without virtue and what it represents human self-definition would be impossible. Every act would be lost in its doing unless we were able to say that the act itself exemplified some virtue. The language of virtue is used not only to evaluate our conduct but also to define ourselves. It supplies the soul with content. Thus, the fact that citizens reflect upon virtue is as important as their reflections themselves. Virtue defines and ranks, and lends stability to who we are. In eliminating virtue, Praxagora eliminates a source of division in the city, but she also eliminates the language of self-understanding. The whole she makes of the city requires individuals to forfeit their ability to make wholes of themselves.

Not only does Praxagora's city eliminate the pride one takes in one's virtue, it also eliminates the pride one takes in one's beloved. There is no longer anyone to whom one says, "*My* dear," or "You belong to me." As Blepyrus demonstrates, he well understands the significance of Praxagora's laws:

> And now the nose of Lysikrates will think itself equal to the beautiful[13] (630).

No longer will the beautiful take pride in themselves. Praxagora's response to Blepyrus takes this further:

> Yes by Apollo, and what's more the decree is democratic, and a great laugh will arise in the face of the upper classes and those donning signet rings, when a man wearing common shoes says speaking ahead of them, "stand aside and look out, for when I have gained my objective I'll give you a second pressing"[14] (631-4).

The measure of Praxagora's agreement with Blepyrus is reflected in the oath that begins her sentence. This is the only time in the play she swears by Apollo. What is more, this is the only time in the play she appeals to the democratic character of her regime. Evidently, beauty represents such a threat that she needs to employ her heavy artillery—Apollo and the demos.

In Aeschylus' *Oresteia*, Apollo represents the attempt to conquer necessity. First, he attempts to absolve Orestes from the necessity of being punished by the Furies for killing Clytemnestra. Then it is revealed at *Eumenides*, 723 that Apollo freed Admetus from the necessity of his own death. By defending Orestes from the condemnation of the Furies, Apollo defends innovation. Thus, Praxagora's invocation of Apollo at the dramatic close of the presentation of her sex laws is fitting. For her sex laws attempt to conquer erotic necessity and are, to say the least, innovative.

While Praxagora's appeal to Apollo is perhaps understandable, her appeal to the people presents a difficulty. Although the easy life and jewelry of the rich gives them an advantage over the poor in appearing beautiful, it is not immediately clear why her sex laws would work against the upper classes, unless it is simply true that the rich are beautiful and the poor ugly. From Praxagora's example, one would think it is the poor not the ugly who are given precedence by Praxagora's sex laws.

Above, Praxagora does something else for the first time. She uses poetry instead of prose. As part of her explanation of her sex laws, she creates a character who before invoking her laws taunts the man whose beloved he is about to bed. The only other time Praxagora does this is again within a demonstration of her sex laws.[15] Interestingly, here too, one of her characters engages in a taunt (706-9). With respect to property, Praxagora's presentation is dispassionate and prosaic. She just says what must be done. With respect to sex, she instigates. Her dramatization highlights not only what the ugly are given, but what the ugly force the beautiful to do without. Her dramatization not only advertises the sexual pleasure her laws make possible, but also what one ought to feel as one invokes her sex laws. Not only do her laws offer the possibility of sexual pleasure, but also the pleasure of satisfied righteous indignation.[16] Sex is not just sex. It is an opportunity for revenge. Why does Praxagora push her citizens in this direction?

Once property is redistributed, wealth is no longer a source of pride and envy. With respect to wealth, Praxagora may achieve perfect equality, but not with respect to beauty. In order to combat the pride and envy which may result from this persisting inequality, Praxagora makes known through her dramatization the opportunity her sex laws present to the ugly. Her laws enable the disadvantaged to avenge themselves. The advantaged are forced to accept "sloppy seconds." They not only have to wait for sex, the sex they get is less desirable. Praxagora's sex laws will be triggered as much by resentment as by sexual desire.

As one reflects upon Praxagora's new city and its sex laws, one wonders why Praxagora needs the sex laws at all. For as Aristophanes enables us to see, there is another way for Praxagora to handle the problem of the natural inequality in looks. Praxagora makes clear that her city for all its egalitarianism will continue to make use of male slaves to work the fields, and prostitutes (female slaves) to gratify these slaves.[17] Why not force the slaves to gratify the ugly? Praxagora could have achieved the same result without having to impose so severe a restriction upon her free citizens. So, why doesn't she? It is with this question in mind that we turn to the hag scene.

Notes

1. See 498-9, 506-516.

2. In order to get relief from his constipation, Blepyrus prays to Ilithyia, the goddess of childbirth (369-71). However, as Strauss points out, the men do not become women. The *Assemblywomen* does not bring about the complete reversal of the conventional gender roles. Praxagora's intention is not to compel the men to assume the responsibilities formerly assumed by women, for this would entail the preservation of the *oikos*, and it is the *oikos* that she wants to annihilate. The Assembly of women is necessarily followed by community of women, for no one is left to preserve the family. Strauss, *Socrates and Aristophanes*, 270.

3. Ussher postulates that he is Chremes. However, at 477, Aristophanes leaves no doubt that Chremes leaves the scene. Having made clear that Chremes has left, Aristophanes, I think, would also have made clear that Chremes has returned, if he had wanted us to know that this speaker is Chremes. Since Aristophanes does not make this clear, I think it is better to assume that our second speaker is no one in particular. In any case, this is also the assumption of the Oxford text.

4. So, *agoreuo* may mean to speak in the Assembly.

5. 675-680.

6. Aristophanes wrote another play in which the women seize control of the city, *Lysistrata*, which is the name of the woman who leads the revolt.

7. See 588-9. Praxagora's presentation of her city in speech resembles her city. For Praxagora in saying she wants no interruptions is saying that she does not wish her speech broken up into parts. It must be allowed to come to light as a whole.

8. Praxagora does not make explicit the subject of her sentence. I assume it is perjury, the subject of Blepyrus' last remark, but the subject may be money, the subject of the first remark. This ambiguity does not make a difference to my argument.

9. The identity of the speaker is not certain. According to the Oxford edition, Blepyrus is the speaker. Ussher, however, gives this line to the other male character on stage who he supposes is Chremes.

10. Kremer has come to the same conclusion. Kremer, *Assemblywomen*, 269.

11. 730-876.

12. *Tattomenon*, above, is derived from the attic verb, *tatto*, which may mean to station in order of battle, or put things in their place. Interestingly, this scene opens with the law-abiding citizen ordering his goods to form a procession so that he can bring them into the agora (730-45). Bowie claims the law-abiding citizen is parodying the Panathenaea with "his parade of household goods." Bowie, *Aristophanes*, 255; see also Strauss, *Socrates and Aristophanes*, 273. All his private things are put into their place before he submits them to the city. Similarly, the city imposes an order on him.

13. The man with the unseemly nose is appropriately named Lysikrates, or, "dissolver of power." Beauty exercises undemocratic power. It is not distributed equally, and justifies our treating some differently than others. Praxagora forces beauty to yield to the legal demands of her revolution. Beauty's power is dissolved.

14. "Second pressing" is a term which applies to wine. The upper classes are forced to stand aside and, as it were, settle for the lees.

15. 693-709.

16. Kremer has drawn a similar conclusion. *Aristophanes*, 263-4.

17. 651, 718-24.

CHAPTER NINE

Praxagora's City of Pigs: The Hag Scene

Judging from the number of lines Aristophanes gives to the hag scene, it is the most important scene of the play. Praxagora's rehearsal speech (171-240) is 70 lines, her proof (583-724) 142 lines, and the hag scene (877-1111) 235 lines. Aristophanes dedicates almost a fifth of his play to a scene which seems to have no relevance to the plot of the play. If it were omitted, it is not easy to understand what would be lost. Praxagora's new city would go on just the same. That the hag scene abstracts from the plot of the play is evidenced by the fact that Praxagora neither appears nor is mentioned. Although her new laws set in motion the action of the scene, she plays no role in directing its action.[1] If the *Assemblywomen* is Aristophanes' thought experiment, and Praxagora its catalyst, then the hag scene might be regarded its logical consequence. It is, as it were, an epilogue. Praxagora is absent from the hag scene because we are being invited to reflect upon Praxagora's product not Praxagora, on the city not its maker. The hag scene is the vantage point from which we are to understand Praxagora's invention as a whole, as is suggested by the anonymity of its participants and the lack of reference to calendar time. Individual personalities do not matter; anyone will do. And the time is irrelevant. It appears to take place on day 1 of Praxagora's city, but it could just as well be day 1000.[2]

The scene opens with an old woman, a hag as later she herself suggests (1017), complaining about being kept waiting as she stands in her doorway (877). Her frustration is compounded by the labor she has expended on her appearance. As she tells us, her face is covered in white lead, and her body in an undoubtedly eye-catching yellow dress. Though she all but admits she is old (896), her make-up and dress suggest she is young. One might say, then, that she is in disguise. The opening of the hag scene thus reminds us of the opening of the play, in which Praxagora disguised as a man is kept waiting by her comrades. Praxagora and her companions' disguises were their Trojan horse by means of which the women gain entrance to the

Assembly and give birth to a new Athens. Praxagora has in mind revolution. As we shall see, so does the hag.

The hag says that while waiting she sings a song to herself "in order to snag any one of the men going by" (880-2).[3] And she pleads with the Muses to put in her mouth an alluring tune. The hag is as indiscriminate in her prayer as she is in her choice of men.[4] Any muse and any man will do. A young woman, immediately appears, as if in spiteful answer to the hag's prayer, and says, "Old crone, you've managed to peep out before me" (884).

Ostensibly, this scene is supposed to demonstrate Praxagora's sex laws in operation; however, the action is not unfolding as Praxagora said it would. First, in describing the types of men who would exploit her sex laws, Praxagora spoke of the "lower," the "ugly," and the "small" (626-9); and the types of women, the "lower," the "more-snub-nosed" and the "ugly" (617-8). Praxagora never said anything about the old. In fact, Praxagora's first pronouncement on her sex laws suggests that she is not thinking about the old at all:

> But it will be possible for him to sleep with her for free. For I am making these women wives in common for the men to sleep and *bear children* (613-5, my emphasis).

Second, in Praxagora's presentation the ugly do not need to adorn themselves with cosmetics or music. They rely upon the allure of another whom they lie beside, and the law (617). The hag peeps out first, but she should peep out second. From what she has said, it is not clear whether she accepts the premise of Praxagora's new regime. It is the compulsion of the law not Eros that is to be invoked. Having lost sight of this, at least for the moment, she accepts the young girl's invitation to a contest in love songs.

After letting fly an insult, the hag sings:

> If anyone wishes to experience something good, it is necessary to lie next to me.[5] For skill (*sophos*) is not in the young but in the ripe. And let me tell you no one would be more willing than I would to love the beloved whoever he happened to be, in contrast to the lover who would fly to another (893-9).

Rather than resort to the law, the hag relies on her merits. She lays claim to skill, which despite the manifest proof of her physical decay makes her as stable as a rock, or a Platonic idea. For she will not desert her beloved for another. The hag wants to accomplish in the realm of Eros what Praxagora accomplishes in the realm of politics. Through skill in manipulation, she will satisfy desire. Just as Praxagora meets the bodily needs of citizens by canceling their aspirations to transcend those needs, so the hag would meet sexual needs by canceling the transcendent character of sex. Praxagora's city is all appetite and no virtue, the hag's view of love all sex and no beauty.

The danger of the hag's view for Praxagora's city can be inferred from the consequences of its success. Its success would force Praxagora to change her laws. Sex would have to be distributed to the inept rather than to the lower, more-snub-nosed[6] and uglier. And since skill is not as transparent as looks, this possibility would pose enforcement difficulties for Praxagora's city. Not only that, if manipulative skill is the root of sex, if sex is all a matter of manipulation, and all the manipulation of matter, the skillful could apply their skill to themselves. The need for the other could be rendered technologically obsolete. That sex is not just this, Praxagora as well as the hag seem to recognize. For Praxagora, as we have seen, uses sex to fuel and satisfy resentment. Sex is not just sex. And the hag's claims about sex are themselves part of her love song, an image she projects to entice an unsuspecting male pedestrian. If images can attract, as the hag seems to believe, then sex is more than physical manipulation. The fact of her love-speech conflicts with its content. Furthermore, despite the hag's self-proclaimed skill, she does not take kindly to the young girl's suggestion that she "go screw herself."[7]

Whether the content or the fact of the hag's love-speech prevails, the hag's words threaten to undermine Praxagora's city. In the former case, if sex is just manipulation, the end result is solitude. There is no envy, because there is no community. In the latter case, if the fact of the hag's love song is taken to its logical extreme, if citizens become lovers of the skillful, as the hag hopes, having skill will carry prestige. A competition will emerge over who is the best. In the latter case, community is preserved but so is envy. Praxagora's dream of a united city goes unrealized.

The illegality of the hag's point of view is reflected by the girl's response:

> Don't envy the young! (900).

The hag wants something she cannot have. She not only wants to be loved, she wants to be recognized as lovable. Therefore she envies the girl. For the girl has what the hag needs to be loveable:

> For femininity grows in my soft body and blooms atop my peaches (901-4).

As the girl suggests, she is able to attract by virtue of her voluptuous body, which apparently is in full bloom (900-4). The hag, by contrast, "laying there having been painted is the beloved of Death" (905). The girl suggests that the hag has nothing any earthly man could want. Moreover, the constancy of her devotion, which the hag trumpets, makes her a perfect match for Death.[8]

Despite the fact that the hag seems doomed, the girl and the hag continue to exchange barbs until a young man appears (906-34). In order to prove to the hag once and for all that she herself is the desirable one, the girl retreats (934-6). The youth's uncoaxed behavior will reveal the girl's desirability and the hag's repulsiveness better than anything she can say. The girl has the confidence of youth, but the hag remains defiant:

> So do I [retreat], so that you know I hold myself in much higher regard than you do[9] (937).

The hag wants recognition. Praxagora's regime is built on the premise that recognition is undemocratic. There is no place in the city for the hag's self-esteem.

Having removed the women from view, Aristophanes now directs our attention to the young man. To the consternation of the hag, the young man immediately proves the girl's point. He makes known that he does not want to be compelled to satisfy a "snub-nosed" or "older" woman before lying with his young beloved (938-40). As he says:

> For this is not endurable for a free man (941).

The youth objects to forced sex. It offends his democratic sense of dignity. The youth seems to object as much to what the act represents as to the act itself.

The youth is as dangerous to Praxagora's city as the hag. More so, for his fall will be the worst of all. Before the day is done, after escaping the bony clutches of this hag, he will succumb to the bony clutches of two others, each more horrible than this first hag. The hag scene, in fact, concludes with the youth's lament, the longest continuous speech of the scene. In it, he calls himself, appropriately, "triply damned," and asks the audience after the hags are through with him to perch the uglier of them, like a tombstone, at the foot of the bed, implying that it is to his grave that he is being dragged (1098-1111). Despite the girl's taunts and the young man's (977, 1030-4, 1079-80), he is the one who ends up dead. Since his death is only symbolic, what is it that dies?

That the young man regards obeying the law an insult is equivalent to a revolt against Praxagora's regime. He regards the city's laws as beneath him. Praxagora's perfectly united regime requires citizens to relinquish talk of above and below. In part, this is what it means to dispense with virtue. What would happen if citizens decided that eating in the common mess was beneath them? Praxagora has a Glaucon on her hands.[10] His reaction to Praxagora's laws is not unlike Glaucon's reaction to Socrates' "healthy" city. Moreover, Praxagora's city from which the youth would like to rebel is not unlike the healthy city. Both are dedicated to the body. Both have no place for virtue. And, as this comparison brings to our attention, both abstract from anger or spiritedness. Glaucon's anger is aroused by Socrates' city, which depicts man as a brute. Unable to contain himself, Glaucon calls it a city of pigs. Glaucon's reaction forces Socrates to do away with his healthy city.[11] The youth's reaction forces Praxagora's healthy city to do away with him.

The problem of spiritedness does not enter here from out of the blue, but first arose much earlier. Praxagora made passing reference to it in her rehearsal speech, when she spoke of the conflict between the moralistic and mercenary citizens—the former want the latter put to death[12]—and in her reference to Thrasyboulos' anger.[13] And in the dialogue between Praxagora and her interlocutors, the problem of spiritedness underlies Praxagora and Blepyrus' discussion of lawsuits (655-75). Blepyrus asks Praxagora how those found guilty will pay their fines. His question is motivated by the fact that since there is no private property, the guilty will have nothing to pay. Praxagora responds by saying there will be no lawsuits. The word she uses for lawsuits, *dikai*, is the plural of *dike*, which may mean justice. Blepyrus is skeptical, offering several reasons why lawsuits will continue. One is particularly revealing. Blepyrus poses the case of an individual being stripped of his cloak (668). To which Praxagora responds, in part, "What is the matter (*pragma*) driving him to fight? For he will take a better one from the common store"(670-1). No one will fight to defend his own, for Praxagora's city literally makes nothing dear. Praxagora pragmatically eliminates fighting, which she takes to be the equivalent of a lawsuit, by defusing spiritedness. For our spiritedness is aroused when what belongs to us is taken away. One may say that Praxagora, whose name is related to the word *pragma*, uses the fruits of *techne*, or abundance, to de-spirit citizens. Lawsuits (justice) disappear, because they are useless or impractical. The overarching justice that Praxagora institutes requires that no citizen strive for justice on his own. In Praxagora's city, justice exists only on the level of the regime. The consequences of this are best revealed by Glaucon. Is not the indifference to being robbed similar to the indifference to eating on the ground?

The young man's response to Praxagora's law is characteristically democratic. For to the democratic man, constraints are more than just constraints, they are insults. Democracy means equality, that is, no one is above me, no one can tell me what to do. This truth about democracy is well captured in the Revolutionary War flag featuring a coiled snake and the caption "Don't tread on me!" Democracy and spiritedness feed off one another. Democracy asserts rights, which give rise to anger in the event of their violation, and aroused anger craves recognition in the form of rights. For an illustration, consider the acronym M.A.D.D. Spiritedness is self-assertive, it asserts the importance of the self. It expresses itself in absolutes such as, "I will not live like a pig," "I refuse to be forced to sleep with hags." It seems inseparable from the standards we set. Praxagora's regime, in turn, attempts to eliminate standards in an effort to unite the people into a homogeneous mass. Therefore, Praxagora's city requires the youth's death. He must be negated, because he will force the city to pursue objectives that will undermine its unity. There can be no order as long as there is aspiration. But does this mean Praxagora's regime attempts to dispense entirely with spiritedness? As the hag scene suggests, to our surprise, no.

Hearing the youth lament the law's demands, the hag says to herself:

> Then by Zeus, you shall wet your beak while wailing. . . . For according to the law doing these things is just, if we are a democracy (942-5).

Having been ignored by the Muses, the hag invokes Zeus, and then lays claim to the law, justice and democracy. Zeus is, among other things, the god of the thunderbolt, which he uses to punish the unjust. Unable to coerce the youth with the power of Eros, the hag is poised to strike him with a bolt of lightning, and take what the law says she has coming to her. Though the hag is loath to admit it, Zeus, not Aphrodite, is now the divinity one must worship in the midst of sexual desire. And yet while the hag appears armed and ready to shoot, she strangely tells us that she will hold her fire (946).[14]

The hag's restraint might be explained away as strategic. She waits for the girl to arouse the youth's lust so as to benefit from it herself. However, as the youth makes clear, he already is lustful:

> Oh gods, that I might seize this beautiful girl alone, having gotten drunk,
> I now head for her being in heat a long time (947-8).

Waiting would appear unnecessary, and the law would seem to sanction her immediate intervention. Yet the hag permits the lovers to converse for 25 lines before she intervenes. Why?

While we reflect on this question, Aristophanes forces us to listen to the love duet of the two lovers. Their love duet stands in stark contrast to the "love speech" of the hag. Whereas the hag's speech is abstract, in that there is nothing in particular to which she is attracted,[15] the lovers each cite specific features in one another that they are drawn to. The girl cites the boy's curls (954-5), the boy the girl's lap and ass (964-5). In identical prayers, each prays to Eros for release and to bring the other to bed, and each sings of the pain of longing the other causes. Each makes reference to Aphrodite who is credited with being the cause of their present miserable condition. The lovers are disciples of Aphrodite. The stage is set for a war between the gods.

After the love duet concludes and both lovers have confessed their pain, the hag intervenes. The timing of the hag's arrest is significant. It exudes ill-intent. She waits for both lovers' desire to boil so as to maximize the impact of her arrest. Like Zeus' thunderbolt, in applying the law the hag inflicts pain. The hag exploits the opportunity that Praxagora has made available—the opportunity to express righteous indignation.[16] At first, however, in keeping with her self-esteem, she refuses to invoke the law. It is the youth not the hag who first employs legalistic language (982-4, 1006-7). Instead, she insists that the youth has been knocking on her door. He denies it, saying that she mistakes him for Sebinos, whose name means "you-the fucker." The hag replies:

> By Aphrodite (yes you are), whether you are willing or not (981).

Having listened to the love duet of the two youths, the hag borrows from it. In their love duet, the youths romanticize their desire. They attribute it to Aphrodite. Aphrodite and Eros compel them. As the hag suggests to the youth, if love is compulsion, then she can compel as well as anyone or any god. Before it was Aphrodite, now it is the law. Unfortunately for the hag, however, no matter how much she swears by Aphrodite, it is clear to the youth that the law is a hag covered in white lead. The law is completely devoid of charm.

Nevertheless, as the youth continues to resist her advances, the hag continues to swear by Aphrodite:

> By Aphrodite, whom I drew by lot at birth, I shall not let you go (999-1000).

As Aphrodite's chosen one she is obliged not to squander this chance at love. But as her speech makes clear, she is a false disciple. Whereas the youths refer to their throbbing bodies, and are drawn to specific features in one another, she says nothing about her own desire, nor anything in the youth to which she is attracted. Aphrodite is the goddess of the particular. For she supports our attraction to a particular someone, and our particular attractiveness to some other. Aphrodite gives truth to what seems to defy truth. For erotic passion defies universalization. Based on the hag's words, there is nothing happening in her as a result of her encounter with the youth which merits Aphrodite's attention. Her "love" is abstracted from the particular. And to suit her purposes, she would convert Aphrodite into the goddess of the ugly abstraction. It bears mentioning at this point, that Praxagora's regime could be instituted anywhere.[17] It too is an ugly abstraction.

In contrast to the hags, the youths are elevated to Aphrodite by what they feel for one another, and, in turn, what they feel for one another is elevated by Aphrodite. To express their desire, the youths speak of what they see then and there. The hag speaks of the remote past—her own birth. Her use of Aphrodite does not lend charm to her desire, it sanctions her use of force.[18]

Despite the hag's lack of success, she makes one final misuse of Aphrodite:

> By Aphrodite, you must sleep with me, as I enjoy bedding men your age (1008-9).

To which the youth responds:

> Whereas I am vexed by women your age, and would never be persuaded (1010-1).

The hag invokes Aphrodite to sanctify the pleasure she takes in sex with young men. She is in love with a category whose representatives—since not all the young are beautiful—include the ugly as well as the beautiful. Her entreaty fails. Neither Aphrodite nor the youth take one step in her direction.

The hag now loses faith in Aphrodite to whom she was never truly faithful. She does not invoke her again. The time has come for Zeus:

> By Zeus, this decree compels you (1013).

The hag points to a written copy of Praxagora's decree, from which in a moment she will read (1015-20). It was the law all along that was the cause of her desire, and so it is to the law that she finally appeals:

> For it is necessary for our laws to be obeyed[19] (1022).

Laws are universals which are applied to the particular. In order for them to function, they must be framed generally, or abstractly, so as to cover a plurality of cases. By design no law will perfectly fit any particular case, for if it should, it would fail to fit every other case, and would be as useless as the particular case to which it is applied is unique. Since no particular case perfectly fits the law, all law does violence to the particular. After the hag reads the law, the youth responds:

> Today I shall become a Procrustes (1021).

Procrustes was a malicious thief who according to myth devised a diabolical method to punish those who crossed his path. He forced one to lie on his iron bed, and cut or stretched as the particular case required to make his victim fit the bed. Like Procrustes the youth is now being forced into a bed, i.e., the law, that does not fit him by a long shot, and which could be made to fit him only through his mutilation.

As this scene suggests, Praxagora's city forces Aphrodite to yield to Zeus, but why Aphrodite is here at all is a question. Why are we being led to the view that Praxagora's city necessitates conflict between Zeus and Aphrodite?

Zeus is the god of order. With power he brings order to heaven and earth. In heaven, his reign ends the parricides that plagued the reign of Ouranos and Kronos. On Earth, he underwrites the law, which brings order to human affairs, by punishing injustice. He is the universal standard the law needs to protect it from the charge that all law is a matter of convention, and therefore may be disobeyed as long as one does not get caught. Without Zeus, the law would be indistinguishable from force, and the world would be awash in relativism. Unlike the hag's decree, Zeus' understanding of justice is obscure; nevertheless he bears some resemblance to Procrustes. The realization of Zeus' universal standard forces all human particularity out of existence. One law for all humankind means order, but at the price of our humanity.

Aphrodite supplies an alternative to Zeus and Praxagora. Whereas Zeus and Praxagora wipe out particularity, Aphrodite justifies our attachment to the particular. Whereas Zeus and Praxagora point to a world state, Aphrodite points to the necessary coldness of that state, and to the idea that the greatest human happiness is not imposed from above, but emerges from below. Zeus and Praxagora's state is the product of instituted laws. It is made, and therefore does not warrant any special feeling. It can be unmade and made again as our understanding of the best model dictates. Aphrodite's attachments are as unique as they are unforgable. They grow, they are not made. Therefore, they are cherished. Zeus and Praxagora's polis is rational but sterile. Its appearance marks the end of history. The final solution has been discovered. Aristophanes' image, the love of hags, perfectly captures the logical conclusion towards which Praxagora's regime leads. Aphrodite represents the unattainability of perfection, a world of growth and aspiration.[20]

Once she is empowered by Zeus, there seems no stopping the hag. The youth's imminent surrender is evident as he lamely asks, "And is this necessary for me?" To which the hag responds,"Yes, a Diomedian necessity" (1030).[21] Thinking all is lost, the youth alludes to his forthcoming death (1030-3), and then his girlfriend enters (1037). She accuses the hag of lacking moderation.[22] For her age would make her a better mother to the youth than a wife (1038-40). As she says,

> So that if you establish this law, you shall fill the whole land with Oedipuses (1041-2).

The girl's allusion to incest sends the hag reeling:

> Oh disgusting woman, you lit upon this speech through envy, but I shall get revenge (1043-4).

The hag then exits. After putting on a face and an alluring dress, summoning the Muses, and participating in a lengthy debate, the hag retires just because the girl cries incest. Why?

One might say the hag flees because as a worshipper of Zeus, she cannot bear to violate the universal prohibition against incest. But if the hag were concerned about committing incest, why does she not inquire into the youth's lineage? The hag asks no questions, and registers no doubt, because there is no doubt that the youth is not her son or even a close relative. She is in no danger of violating the universal law against incest. So why does she flee? The hag does not flee from the fact of incest—Zeus' concern—but, it would seem, from the image of incest—Aphrodite's concern. Aphrodite is concerned with images, or appearances, as the hag herself suggests with her turn to both cosmetics and music. The girl exploits the inherent ugliness of incest to scare away the hag. The girl's reference to incest spoils the hag's mood. Through luck or brilliance, the girl exploits the hag's dual allegiance to Aphrodite and Zeus. The hag wants eros, but she must settle for state-mandated sex. She wants recognition for being lovable, but there is nothing loveable about her, so she must invoke the law.

The youth now, joyously but ominously exclaims,

> By Zeus, the savior, you have made me happy (1045).

The youth has reason to be happy, but no reason to be grateful to Zeus. For Aphrodite not Zeus saved him. If Zeus had anything to do with the hag's sudden departure, it was only to inflict a fate far worse.

No sooner is the youth free of the first hag than he is beset by an even uglier one (1049-53). And, soon after, one uglier still (1065-73). Unlike hag number one, hags two and three have no interest in Aphrodite. They never swear by her; they call upon no Muse; they make no reference to their skill or wisdom, or anything appealing in themselves; they, in fact, appeal to their ugliness not their beauty (1077-8); they do not even mention their desire. They base their claim only upon the law (1049-51, 1055-6, 1077-8), which they embody. As hag number two says,

> It is not I, but the law which drags you (1055-6).

They are self-righteousness incarnate. Needless to say, they will not be repelled by images of incest. Zeus is the god to whom they appeal (1085,1088), which is in keeping with the reason the hags are on stage.[23] They are on stage to inflict a punishment that the first hag could not bring herself to inflict. It would make sense, though it is hard to prove, that the appearance of hags 2 and 3 on the stage is precisely that revenge which hag 1 promised as she exited. Hag 1 has the law on her side, but cannot stomach its execution. So she summons hags 2 and 3 who do have a stomach for its execution. If hag 1 takes no pleasure in executing the law herself, at least she takes pleasure in knowing that justice is served. In the end, she outwits her young rival, and gets the revenge she swore she would get.[24]

Long after Praxagora's laws have leveled wealth and produced a classless society, how will Praxagora maintain among its citizens a devotion for the regime?

Praxagora's sex laws are her admission that every regime needs a defense of itself. It needs manifest proof of its justice. Without material inequality or hunger, the very question of justice would slip away. Praxagora's sex laws enable citizens to experience the goodness of justice, or the justice of her regime every time they are employed. Sex becomes an entirely political act.[25] It is the symbol of Praxagora's ability to bring the transcendent beauty of democracy down to Earth. For now democracy's most illustrious mottoes are not just stamped on dollar bills to remind us of democracy's aspirations. They are experienced every time genitalia are forced together. They come down to Earth also in that they serve an earthly function, maintaining a spirited love for the regime. That the means used to keep this spirit alive are fantastic is Aristophanes' implicit admission that Praxagorian communism is impossible. We have seen several examples of communism in history, but no examples of Praxagora's sex laws—an ingenious device for keeping spirit alive while keeping it in check. Since there will always be the old and the young, there will always be resentment between them. And as long as this resentment is satisfied in the time it takes to consummate sex, it cannot work any mischief, not even children.

Notes

1. One can make the same case for the previous scene, the confrontation between the un-law-abiding and law-abiding citizen (730-876). However, there a "heraldess" intrudes (834-52). In the hag scene neither Praxagora nor her emissaries appear.

2. At 988, the first hag refers to the fact that the youth has had dinner. In the closing scene of the play, Blepyrus is said to be the happiest citizen because he is the only one who has not yet eaten. None of this contradicts my claims for the hag scene.

3. Cf. 930-1.

4. Cf. Strauss, *Socrates and Aristophanes*, 275.

5. Cf. 699-701.

6. Translates *phaulos* and *simos* in 617.

7. The girl's suggestion is at 915-17. The hag's response is at 918-23.

8. Cf. *Antigone*. At 816, Antigone proclaims that she will be the bride of Acheron, a river in Hades.

9. Cf. 630.

10. The parallels between Socrates' healthy city and Praxagora's gynecocracy are many. Socrates' healthy city originates in need and climaxes in need (369b4-6; 372a1-2). It begins because each man is not autarchic, and concludes with Adeimantus' definition of justice as the need citizens have of one another. By my count *dei* and *chre* (both of which may mean, it is necessary) and words derived therefrom occur sixteen times in Socrates' presentation of the healthy city. In Praxagora's rehearsal speech, words derived from *chraomai* appear eleven times. Praxagora's city, like Socrates', is steeped in need. In addition, both Socrates and Praxagora's cities are technocratic. Socrates' city is based on the principle of one man one art. Praxagora's is based on the artistic proficiency of women,

and of her regime. In Greek, *techne* is a feminine noun. Praxagora's city does not require active intelligence, for like a perfectly engineered machine, it is presumed that it can run on its own.

11. As a replacement, Socrates first offers Glaucon a luxurious city. Like the city of pigs, it is dedicated to appetite, but unlike the city of pigs it qualifies the manner in which the appetites are satisfied. Glaucon demands couches and tables. He does not want to eat on the ground. However, Glaucon is not really interested even in this. For Socrates really grabs Glaucon's attention with the image of a guardian, which Glaucon then aspires to become. The guardians' standard of living makes that of the city of pigs look luxurious. Glaucon is not interested in a high standard of living. Glaucon wants recognition.

12. Lines 187-8. See p. 77 and p. 81, above.

13. Lines 202-3. See p. 81, above.

14. Although the hag recognizes that the law is on her side, for some reason she chooses not to invoke it. In 946, she tells us she will continue to observe. Thus "she holds her fire." She is not ready to hurl Zeus' thunderbolt.

15. Recall, any Muse and any man will do.

16. The Athens of the *Knights* is ablaze in righteous indignation. Lawsuits abound, because of the violent-tempered Paphlagon and the character of democracy. Democracy is based on an idea or principle (equality), and so the appeal to principle that is made in a lawsuit is appealing to democratic ears. Athenian litigiousness is a recurrent theme in Aristophanes' plays, and is the central theme of the *Wasps*. The sausage-seller wants to move Demos away from politics, so it is no accident that whereas Paphlagon encourages political conflict, the sausage-seller gets Demos to accept peace terms. Rather than encourage Demos to prosecute a war by reference to injustice, the sausage-seller gets Demos to stop fighting by invoking the charms of private life. While Praxagora also attempts to combat Athenian litigiousness, as my analysis of the hag scene will show, she needs to retain Athenian spiritedness.

17. In the debate between the un-law-abiding and law-abiding citizen, the un-law-abiding citizen attempts to convince the law-abiding citizen of the stupidity of handing in his goods by arguing that "this is not customary (*patrion*), but it is necessary for us only to take" (778-9). In light of the above, his remark should not be dismissed as an idle joke. Praxagora's regime is the ugly abstraction which wipes out Athenian particularity.

18. Aristophanes foreshadows this by introducing the possibility of forced sex much earlier in the play (465-72).

19. See p. 87, above.

20. Cf. Aristophanes' *Birds*, 695-7. The parabasis of the Birds is a parody of Hesiod's *Theogony*. According to the theogony of the Birds, "Black-winged Night" laid a wind-egg, from which Eros was born. Eros, in turn, couples with Chaos, giving birth to all species of birds.

As Socrates says in Plato's *Minos*, "The law no less wants to be the discovery of that which is" (315a3ff, Benardete translation). This is to say that the law does not want to be the discovery of that which becomes. Becoming, or generation, is the enemy of law. In a few moments, this conflict between the law and generation comes to the fore when the young girl accuses the hag of making the world overflow with Oedipuses. Oedipus sleeps with his mother, and, at least symbolically, tries to become his own maker. You can say that incest represents our resentment at having to be generated. According to Arlene Saxonhouse, by alluding to incest Aristophanes is showing us the consequence of blurring the distinction between the private and the public, or the family and the city. "Incest may have been at first lightly ignored as the impious consequence of the earlier drive to unify the public and the private." Saxonhouse, *Diversity*, 18, see also 14-19. While I think Saxonhouse is right, I would add that Aristophanes alludes to incest because the perfection of the law requires the annihilation of becoming. Recall that Athena, the patron goddess of Athens, emerges whole from Zeus' head.

21. Cf. 493d, Plato's *Republic*. In Bloom's translation, 173, and his note 12.

22. *Sophrosune*, 1038. At 937, 1000 and 1038, notice Aristophanes' use of *phren* or its derivatives. At 937, the hag says, "I would have you know that I hold myself in much higher regard (*phrono*) than you do." Cf. 630. At 1000, the youth tells the hag, "Oh, little old hag, you are insane (*para-**phroneis***)." At 1038, "You are not being moderate (***sophron**-ousa*)."

23. Although in their last utterance of the scene, the uglier of the two hags swears by Hecate, "the mistress of ghosts and of everything dark and uncanny" (E.D. Phillips). She also has a connection with the underworld or with death, for she alone hears Persephone's cries as the latter is carried off into the underworld by Pluto (god of wealth and Hades). Hecate is "always a goddess of private rather than public cult." Bowie, *Aristophanes*, 277, quoting from M.L. West's *Hesiod: Theogony, edited with prolegomena and commentary*, 1966.

24. Ussher says, "we are not to look for fulfillment of this threat in the play." *Ecclesiazusae*, 220, with respect to 1043-4. But given the vengeful character of Praxagora's sex laws, it seems to me that hags 2 and 3 must be regarded as hag 1's revenge.

25. In the *Knights*, there is a flight from the political. In the *Assemblywomen*, everything is political—even sex. One might say, this is what it means for the women to take over the Assembly. Thus, I disagree with Foley. For her the significance of the hag scene is that "competition does not disappear, but is eroticized" (Foley, "Women," 5). While I agree that competition has not disappeared, the point of the scene is to show that eros has been politicized, which is to say that it has been destroyed. As Praxagora's soliloquy opening the play suggest, Eros requires the private light of Praxagora's lamp, and is destroyed by the public light of the sun (Helios). We note in passing that Helios' office was taken over by Apollo whose name in the accusative is very similar to *apollumi*, to destroy. Praxagora refers to her lamp as a signal flame (6). Not only does it signal her fellow conspirators, it signals the conclusion to which her plan ineluctably leads.

CHAPTER TEN

The Political Allegory of the *Assemblywomen*

As we have seen, in Praxagora's rehearsal speech (171-240), Praxagora argues that Athens' poor condition is the result of poor leadership. Athens' leaders pursue their own good rather than the city's. Praxagora implies that the laws themselves are to blame. In particular, she blames the law[1] paying citizens to attend the Assembly:

> For despite being paid from the public treasury, you all look to the private, each the thing he acquires, and the common . . . goes astray (206-8).

Apparently, according to Praxagora, the practice of paying assembly-goers results in citizens who participate in politics solely, or primarily, for the benefit of themselves, to the detriment of the city. Although here Praxagora implies that laws, in part, create men, she well knows that men also create laws. The laws once they give birth to radical self-interest are themselves corrupted by the disposition they induce.

Praxagora turns the city over to women, in part, to arrest this degenerative cycle. In elevating women into politics she exploits women's lack of exposure to the disease of Athenian politics. At the same time, she exploits the habituation that family life affords women. Unlike Athenian men, Athenian women are not addicted to novelty. Instead they are old-fashioned. Unlike Athenian men, they do not long for honor or recognition, which is productive of discord. And, unlike the men, the Athenian women are used to thinking of others and to managing resources so as to provide for bodily needs. The habituation that women have received, conservativism, indifference to honor, sympathy, and economics (properly understood) is exactly what is called for, and all that the city needs, or so Praxagora gets her comrades to believe.

After Praxagora and her comrades depart for the Assembly where Praxagora will become leader of Athens, Aristophanes, instead of allowing us to witness this, introduces us to Blepyrus. While Praxagora is at the Assembly dressed as a man and absorbed by problems of state, Blepyrus is outside his house dressed as a woman absorbed by his own constipation. The contrast Aristophanes has drawn between them is unmistakable. Whereas in the opening scene of the play, Praxagora seeks light, here, Blepyrus seeks darkness (320-322). Whereas Praxagora longs for and is able to transcend the limits of her body in that she is able to both look like a man, and perform a very manly act, obtaining control of Athens, Blepyrus is trapped by his body. Whereas Praxagora is concerned about the welfare of Athens, Blepyrus is concerned only about the pay he will receive if he is admitted to the Assembly (380, 392).

The contrast Aristophanes creates between Praxagora and Blepyrus helps us identify the essential traits that distinguish the one from the other. Praxagora is noble, patriotic and resourceful. Blepyrus is base, selfish and inept. He cares only for the needs of his own body. Even his desire to ease himself is based on his single-minded devotion to his body.

> By Dionysus, I am really tied up. But what shall I do? For not even is this the only thing which troubles me; but to know where the dung will go to in the future, when I eat (357-360).

Evidently, his desire to free himself from bodily constraint is inspired by a demand of the body, eating. Furthermore, he is not worried that his constipation may prevent him from serving his civic duty in that its continuation will cause him to miss the Assembly. Blepyrus epitomizes the Athens of which Praxagora has spoken and the men which she and her comrades have criticized.

That Blepyrus represents the old Athens is implied by Praxagora herself in her opening remarks to the Assembly where, posing as a man, she criticizes Blepyrus in particular (Praxagora's remarks are reported by Chremes):

> B: Why, what did he say?
> C: First he said you were a knave.
> B: And what about you?
> C: Don't ask this yet. And then a thief.
> B: I only?
> C: And, by Zeus, an informer too.
> B: I only?
> C: And, by Zeus, most of these [i.e., the audience] (436-440).

Here, Praxagora treats Blepyrus as a proxy for Athenian men as a whole. He embodies the essence of the status quo, the Athens she will attempt to reform. The old Athens seems to be a reflection of Blepyrus. He is perfectly at home in it. Its lack of standards suits his inability to live up to any, and the low existence it offers suits his base desires. In judging Praxagora's reforms, we must question whether her reforms elevate, leave untouched, or further debase men like Blepyrus. The answer to this question suggests whether her reforms represent revolution or further regression.

It is clear from Praxagora's first promise as Athens' leader that she will change Athens. She promises that:

> no longer by means of boldness will the city herself do shameful things,
> no giving evidence, no informing (560-2).

Right at this point Blepyrus stridently objects.[2] Blepyrus does not like Praxagora's new city because the termination of Athens' shameful life means, evidently, the termination of Blepyrus' shameful living. He will no longer be able to satisfy his appetites in his accustomed way. Her proposal interferes with his appetites, because it will impose a standard, or principle, that will make obsolete his occupation. The days of libertarian Athens are over.

As becomes evident, Praxagora brings this about by implementing communism. Athens will be a city at harmony with itself, because everyone will have an adequate and equal share of everything, even sex. No one will be driven by hunger to act shamefully against the state; and, no one will be driven by hunger, or envy, to act against one another (605-606). Bleyprus, however, the hero of the appetitive Athens of yesterday, is not satisfied. He notes that experience teaches that even those with sufficient resources often seek more (607-608). Moreover, appetite is not satisfied by equality, nor is it likely to be satisfied by a fixed ration, because appetite grows with time. The more it gets, the more it wants. As an example, Blepyrus cites sex.

According to Blepyrus, the desire for sex will undermine Praxagora's communism. Blepyrus suggests that wealth attracts lovers, and the more wealth one has the more beautiful the lovers wealth attracts (611-6). The desire for sex will induce men to resist Praxagora's communistic laws. Apparently, Blepyrus accepts the ability of Praxagora's communism to satisfy material needs. He raises no objection about this. Merely, distribute enough food and clothing, and base Athenian men will be content, at least with respect to hunger and warmth. Sex poses a more difficult problem. Blepyrus wonders, as do we, how is this to be distributed? Moreover, how does one equally distribute pleasure? Unlike the appetite for food, which is limited by the body, the appetite for sexual pleasure is elastic.[3] The phenomenon of sexual pleasure threatens Praxagora's entire plan. To the extent property is a means to pleasure, Athenian men will not forfeit their property or accept a merely equal distribution. Blepyrus, the expert on appetite, has confronted Praxagora with a difficult problem. As we shall see, she is equal to it.

Praxagora meets Blepyrus' objection by inventing a "sin tax." Men and women, in order to have sex with their beloved, must first offer sex to an ugly person of the opposite sex who desires it (617-8, 626-629). Praxagora's invention is ingenious, because with one stroke she solves two problems. First, she insures sexual pleasure will be distributed to the ugly and the beautiful. The city is now even more equal. Second, she has devised a way to curb the appetite for sex. Her law imposes a tax on sex, therefore sex will occur less frequently. Sex with the ugly is the tax all the non-ugly must pay in order to have sex with a beloved. Sex will occur less frequently, because such is the effect of taxation. It rarely fails to reduce consumption.

Praxagora's law not only more equally distributes sex. It also places a curb on this dangerous passion. For even if Athenians are not dissuaded from sex by the nature of the tax, there is only so much tax, so to speak, that a man can afford to pay. This tax and the other economic regulations Praxagora has devised give her regime a great deal of control over the actions of men. Athens will no longer be at the mercy of the base desires of men. No longer will the irrational, animal passions of men be allowed to threaten the city. If men consume more food and use more clothing than is healthy for them, or that the city can safely provide, Praxagora can cut their ration. If men are having too much sex, if the population is becoming too large for her city to feed and clothe, the sex tax can be increased. During Praxagora's rehearsal speech she praised women and predicted that they would make great leaders because women are natural economists (211-2, 236-8). Her laws on property and sex are the manifestation of this natural ability.

Blepyrus, at first, objects to Praxagora's sex law, but soon changes his mind, once Praxagora convinces him that it is to his benefit. She points out that he will be collecting the tax, not paying it (619-30). Blepyrus, the personification of the old Athens, is now convinced that Praxagora's reforms will satisfy his appetites.

The remainder of the dialogue reaffirms that Praxagora's Athens will be a united city. There will be no strife. Even her sex laws promote unity:

> P: The uglier and more snub-nosed women shall sit by the side of the beautiful; and then if any desire her, he shall first lie with the ugly one (617-8).

Praxagora portrays her sex laws as promoting unity, and friendliness. The beautiful will not spurn the company of the ugly, despite the fact that the presence of the ugly interferes with their pleasure. Their proximity is no occasion for conflict. Like cattle they graze on the same grass, peacefully.

Blepyrus points out that Praxagora's laws will result in the destruction of the family, and universal enmity, because now no one will be regarded as one's own (635-40). Praxagora's response is that the exact opposite will occur: everyone will be regarded as one's own. Citizens will not be driven to hate one another, but will be drawn together (641-3). Moreover, because property will be distributed to all there will be no feuding over property. Lawsuits will disappear. Courts will become unnecessary, as will the Assembly. Praxagora converts the buildings of state into huge dining halls where everyone will dine. Athens will be so unified there will be no controversies for the state to reconcile. Instead of facilitating conflict, Athens' court house—the site of the common mess—will now facilitate unity. There is nothing left to deliberate over or disagree about.

Praxagora will give Athens a very different look. Praxagora's city eliminates poverty and inequality, and the strife that accompanies them. In addition, Athens will no longer be a city of libertarian freedom. Unlike the old Athens, citizens who do not obey the laws, or who, like Blepyrus, seek to profit at the expense of the state will be punished (665-6). Furthermore, Praxagora introduces shame. Praxagora will appoint a chorus of boys:

> to sing of those who are brave in war, and of him, whoever has been cowardly, so that they may not dine, through shame (677-80).

Needs will be met, but there will be compulsion. Citizens will be forced to observe the sex laws (689-710).

Praxagora eliminates political participation, but its elimination has enabled her to address a flaw of the old Athens—ephemeral laws. By disbanding the Assembly, Praxagora ensures that her laws will endure. Athens will never again be governed by the whims of the old Assembly and its men.

Praxagora's regime represents the conquest of chance. During the rehearsal session, one of Praxagora's comrades, before beginning her mock speech, asks for a drink. After Praxagora scolds her, she asserts that drinking is customary at the Assembly for:

> their decrees, as many as they make are, to people considering well, mad ones, like drunken people's (137-139).

Although the woman's request for a drink is ridiculous and would have endangered their cause if made in the Assembly, her explanation is revealing. Athens' public policy is as unpredictable as the town drunk. Athenian men are governed by appetite, which helps account for their ephemeral laws. Laws based on appetite are not only ephemeral, they are random. They are the manifestation of whatever whim currently occupies Athens' Assembly. Thus, the woman's comment reflects a fundamental flaw of the old Athens. The laws and practices of the old Athens, indeed, make it look drunk. It is being guided by a multitude of whims which cannot possibly sum into a coherent whole. In replacing this multitude of whims with her sound mind, Praxagora flushes chance with reason.[4]

There is much that will change in Athens, if Praxagora implements her program. And yet, even if her city in speech becomes everything she says it will, even if it lives up to her highest expectation, one of the play's greatest ironies is that her city and the one it replaces will remain substantially similar.

In the Athens of old, male appetite is not moderated by a concern for the common good. Justice plays no part in the regime. Moreover, judgment is not exercised. For Athenian public policy is adrift. It does not seem capable of reconciling conflict between the private and the public, or distinguishing good change from bad. The libertarianism of the old Athens might be corrected by judgment, or statesmanship. Instead, Praxagora introduces rations and punishments. Rather than a means for inculcating the virtues of the fully developed human being, Praxagora treats lawbreakers as if they were disobedient children: when you are good, you eat; when you are bad, you do not.

In that Praxagora has eliminated political deliberation, it is difficult to see how it constitutes an improvement on its predecessor. It is true that in the old Athens deliberation was directed towards private rather than public ends, but at least there was deliberation. As long as deliberation remains, the possibility of justice remains. For without at least a concern for justice, concern that manifests itself in deliberation over the public good, how can a city become more just? Moreover, the continued existence of deliberation provides for the continued development of reason. Reason benefits politics, in that it helps guide us towards justice; and, politics induces citizens to cultivate reason, for politics presents human beings with difficult questions. In eliminating deliberation from her regime, Praxagora removes justice from it. She also facilitates the regression of Athenians into primitive quasi-rational beings.

Aristophanes' play is testimony to the educative power of politics. Throughout the play Aristophanes offers many examples of the impact politics has upon human virtue. Politics is able to both educate and corrupt. Praxagora and the chorus point to the regression undergone by Athenian men between the time of Myronides and the time of Agyrrhius (300-10), blaming this regression on the corrupting influence of the law. Before our eyes Praxagora's entourage from bumbling fools become shrewd and brave. Entering the political arena has had an impact upon them. Perhaps the best proof that Aristophanes views politics as the field of human education, or change, are the women themselves. For how have they remained free of the vices plaguing the men? Almost all the men we meet are selfish and ineffective, whereas the women are patriotic and resourceful. It seems that home life has shielded them from the corruptive influence of Athens' politics. They have remained, as they put it, addicted to ancient ways and opinions. The one exception is Praxagora. She was led by circumstances into the political arena, which, according to her, accounts for her ability. Praxagora when asked by a comrade to account for her rhetorical skill says:

> During the flight I dwelt with my husband in the Pnyx; and then listening to the speakers I became conversant in speaking (243-4).

Athenian political life, and perhaps all genuine political life, is constant motion. It facilitates change; it educates or corrupts. In eliminating politics, Praxagora not only does not reform Athenian men; she ensures the permanence of their presently corrupt state.

The movement from Blepyrus' regime to Praxagora's represents a regression, because it seems to make unnecessary even the minimal public virtue present in Blepyrus' Athens. As corrupt as this Athens was, at least citizens retain the ability to reflect and consider, evidenced by Blepyrus in the dialogue with Praxagora. This ability must be sacrificed to the cause of Praxagora's motionless city. Its complete lack of motion represents the ultimate conquest of chance. Chance has been eliminated but the price is high. Citizens lose freedom and the qualities that distinguish us from beasts.[5]

Aristophanes shows us that ephemeral laws are to be preferred to permanent laws, because ephemeral laws leave room for human judgment and deliberation. Praxagora's Athens also shows us that a disunited city is to be preferred to a perfectly united city. Blepyrus' disunited city at least has some form of love, friendship and family. Praxagora's perfectly united city threatens all three.

Praxagora's sex laws require the love-struck to have sex with the ugly, and in doing so sever the link between love and sex. Sex with the ugly occurs without love. But what impact does sex with the ugly have upon love? It seems that love is fueled by two human qualities: our perception of the beautiful, and our physical appetite. When we are in love, both are present. Take either away, and eros evaporates. Praxagora's sex laws take appetite away from eros, thereby threatening eros. The "love affair" will no longer be recognized as the special province of sex. Praxagora makes sex into a commodity that is equally distributed just like everything else. Sex is universally distributed, but it is cheapened.

The love affair is not the only human association that Praxagora's laws threaten. Her laws also cheapen friendship. Praxagora's Athens converts the buildings of state into huge dining halls, in which all are assigned a place by lot[6] (681-7). Thus, chance has reemerged even in her regime of reason. Chance has replaced choice. Athenian men will no longer be able to dine with friends. They must accept the luck of the draw. However, human beings are not drawn to just anyone. They enjoy and are made happy by the company of particular individuals. Just as Praxagora assumes Athenians will be happy having sex with anyone, she also assumes that they enjoy the company of anyone. In the interest of unifying Athens, she compels Athenians to relinquish the particular associations that, while dividing the city, make possible human happiness.

In the interest of crafting the perfectly united city, Praxagora also destroys the family. As Praxagora says, "sons will recognize their elders to be all their own fathers" (636-7). They consider all men to be their fathers. But sons do not want to consider all men their fathers. They want their own fathers. Sons value fathers, in part, because fathers have something to teach them about who they are. Praxagora assumes Athenians are homogeneous, but they are not. Fathers have important knowledge about their sons, which the average stranger does not have. As already noted, she implied that Athenians will be content with sex and companionship regardless of the source. Here, she assumes that the fatherly affection Athenians crave does not require real fathers. Anyone can supply it.

The final episodes of the play leave no room for doubt regarding Aristophanes' view of Praxagora's plan. In the first episode, which we have examined in part in chapter 8, Aristophanes suggests that Praxagora's city in speech will not live up to its predictions. Here, two citizens argue over whether to obey Praxagora's laws. One citizen will obey, one will not. One will seek to benefit from the city's property, without having to relinquish his own. Such an attitude spells disaster for Praxagora's city, because if enough citizens act like the disobedient citizen, Praxagora's communitarian economy will be no more successful than those of our time. Poverty and inequality may be just as prevalent in her city as it is in contemporary communistic regimes.

In the second episode, we learn that that the new Athens also has not rid itself of shamefulness. In our first meeting with Blepyrus, we are given a disgusting image of the depraved state to which Athens has regressed. At the end of the play, although it did not seem possible, we get an even more disgusting image.[7] Three old hags, one uglier than the next, fight for sex from a young lover who longs for his beloved. The unity that Praxagora had promised has not materialized, apparently belying her foresight. Strife remains, but it has taken on a lower form. Before it was over economic issues, now it is over sex. And, the conflict appears even nastier.

Praxagora's city eliminates neither shameful acts nor dissension. Nor is it likely to eliminate poverty and inequality. More importantly, it does not reform Athenian citizens. It represents regression, not revolution. This is implied in the dialogue between Blepyrus and Praxagora to which we have referred. Blepyrus is easily persuaded to accept Praxagora's new regime. The old regime and the new have no serious disagreement with one another. One flows into the other. Blepyrus' Athens has paved the way for Praxagora's. Praxagora's regime is the true regime of the appetitive man. Here, nothing but appetite need concern him.

By making Blepyrus' Athens easily regress into Praxagora's, Aristophanes suggests that a democracy of libertarian freedom may not be as far removed from a democracy of authoritarian egalitarianism as one might think.[8] In moving from the Athens of Blepyrus to the Athens of Praxagora we move from one extreme form of democracy to another, but as the play reveals the cities are not separated by very much distance. Aristophanes suggests that a regime of free choice, equal right of participation, equal opportunity and a laissez-faire government is closely related to a regime of completely equal rations, comprehensive and rigid laws and no participation. In showing us the ease with which Blepyrus' regime gives way to Praxagora's, Aristophanes reveals that although these regimes may have different exteriors, their interiors, or their principles, have much in common.

Not only does the new Athens embody the same principles as the old, it embodies these principles in their perfected form. The old Athens had libertarian freedom and equal participation, but it had inequality and poverty, which implied that it inhibited at least some from the free satisfaction of appetite. Praxagora's Athens provides the freedom that Blepyrus' lacked in enabling all citizens, the ugly and the simple, to enjoy all of life's bodily pleasures. Blepyrus' Athens provides a right of equal participation. But just as our right of equal opportunity does not produce equal results, neither does theirs. Inequality persists. Praxagora's Athens provides the equality that Blepyrus' had in name only. So, Praxagora's Athens embodies the same ideas as Blepyrus', but in a perfected form. Freedom is perfected in that all are free to pursue appetite.[9] And, equality is perfected in that citizens are provided with actual as opposed to potential equality.

Aristophanes has anticipated the two modern forms of democracy. The first is the democracy of the right: it has freedom, participation and equality of opportunity—the old Athens. The second is the democracy of the left: it is authoritarian, denies participation, but offers equality of results and guaranteed material and physical pleasure—the new Athens. Aristophanes' play reveals that both extremes are degrading. Both produce degraded human beings. Both produce only a low form of freedom that has enslavement to body at its core. And, both produce an equality that has most unfortunate side effects. The equality of the right encourages disunity. Individuals use the equal opportunity they have to further their own interests, which increases inequality and makes it difficult to craft policy for the common good. The equality of the left encourages a political unity which has no room for non-political associations like friendship and family. Everything is subordinated to the principle the city tries to impose.

In showing us that both of the great democratic alternatives are deficient, Aristophanes calls to mind the deficiency of their guiding principles, freedom and equality. He suggests that both the democracy of the right and that of the left adopt a low view of freedom. Freedom comes to mean complete absorption to bodily appetite. Democratic man becomes a comic figure in that he does not realize that the freedom he pursues is impossible. Once one is freed from one appetite, another soon rises to take its place. To make matters more comic, if he could free himself from appetite, he would become unhappy, because he would have nothing left to do.[10] Equality, too, is problematic. On the right, it leads to perfect disunity. On the left, it leads to the homogenization of human life.

Aristophanes' Last Word

In the closing scene of the play, Aristophanes has the chorus make a speech to the judges regarding how they ought to judge his play.

> I wish to make a slight suggestion to the judges: to the clever to prefer me, remembering my clever parts; to those who laugh merrily, to prefer me on account of my jokes. Therefore of course I bid almost all to prefer me; and that my lot should not be any cause of detriment to me, because I obtained it first[11]; but they ought to remember all these things and not violate their oaths, but always judge the chorus rightly; and not to resemble in their manners the vile harlots, who remember only whoever happen to be the last comers (1154-1162).

Although we do not know how the judges received Aristophanes' advice, it is hard to believe it was intended for their ears only. For the advice he gives to the judges would seem to apply also to Praxagora's city, and to any democracy for that matter. For if equality is the principle towards which democracy aims, every democracy is headed in the *Assemblywomen*'s direction. He tells the judges of his play and all future democracies, i.e., all citizens, "remember your oath." Look not to equality, look to a transcendent principle.[12] Equality is not only a standard to be applied, but a standard to be judged. Its justice is limited. The unselfconscious application of equality to political life would do to political life what Aristophanes fears it may do to his play: that is, rank it based upon the order in which it was presented, which he says is determined by lot, rather than upon its merits. Furthermore, the unqualified application of equality would make of a comedy what Praxagora's women have made of cuisine[13]—a hodge-podge of indiscernible parts. For if equality is an unmitigated good, what grounds are there for discerning parts or for objecting to the lot as the basis for awarding first prize in a drama contest? If all parts and all plays are equal, choosing by lot is the way to go, for it insures that nothing gets special treatment, or is arranged in a specific order. Democracy's radical tendencies spell the doom of Aristophanes' craft as well as meaningful political life. Extreme equality collapses together the serious and the unserious, the tragic and the comic. As the *Assemblywomen* suggests, Aristophanes' craft is dependent upon the survival of tragedy, for tragedy serves as its foundation.[14]

Notes

1. Thus, the cause of Athens' lamentable situation is the law. In the scene which corresponds to Praxagora's rehearsal speech in the *Knights*, Demosthenes' speech to the audience, Demosthenes blames Paphlagon. Demosthenes blames rule, Praxagora blames the law.

2. 562-3.

3. Of course, this is true of our appetite for food also. Eating is a pleasure as well as a necessity. However, our appetite for food is more constrained by the limits of the body than is our appetite for sex. Therefore, in the regime that attempts to regulate the appetites in order to ensure equality, sex represents the more difficult problem.

4. In the *Knights*, it is the ruler of the people who is drunk. In the *Assemblywomen*, it is the assembly—the lawmakers.

5. The end towards which the *Assemblywomen* leads is not the same as that of the *Knights*. In the *Knights*, Demos in leaving the political arena is no longer subject to its restrictions. Demos re-acquires a natural freedom of sorts. In the *Assemblywomen*, the citizens are induced to accept the most denaturing conventions.

6. One might say that the beginning of the revolution of the *Assemblywomen* is utterly artful, while its end is to some extent random. The *Knights* is the opposite. Its beginning is utterly random, while its end is utterly artful. As the savior of the city, Demosthenes and Nicias recruit the first sausage-seller who passes by. However, at the end of the play, the sausage-seller wondrously returns Demos to youth. That Aristophanes permits us to see that Praxagora's artful city ultimately allows in chance is further evidence, if any were necessary, that he does not approve of Praxagora's city.

7. This suggests another point of contrast between the *Assemblywomen* and the *Knights*. The *Assemblywomen* begins with a beautiful image: the burnished-up Athens of Praxagora's rehearsal speech—Athens unified and public-spirited. But the play ends with a decidedly disgusting image: sex in the street between the old and the young. The new Athens is even more disgusting than the old Athens, a magnificent feat since the old Athens is symbolized by Blepyrus who we first meet squatting constipated in the street. By contrast, the *Knights* begins with a disgusting image (which we are not permitted to see) of Cleon smelling of alcohol and his last meal, lying drunk, farting and snoring atop a bed of animal skins (103-4, 115-7). But the play ends with the sausage-seller and Demos sumptuously attired and Demos made beautiful again. The contrast is not without significance. The disgusting image with which the *Assemblywomen* ends is the consequence of the private made public or of absolute equality. The beautiful image with which the *Knights* ends has to do with the glorification of the private realm or of nature, which the sausage-seller represents.

8. In the play, it is the law which is authoritarian. It is a tyranny by law not men.

9. I mean freedom in the vulgar Marxist sense: a freedom of access not of choice.

10. Cf. the conclusion of Alcibiades' speech in the *Symposium*.

11. Aristophanes is asking the judges not to let their judgment be affected by the order in which the plays are presented, an order determined by lot.

12. He has just said remember your oath.

13. In this scene, Blepyrus is offered a meal that is a composite of an enormous variety of foods. The word that Aristophanes uses to describe it calls to our attention the monstrous

character of this meal. It is the longest word we know of in Ancient Greek literature, as the names for a host of edibles are merged into one. Here we see the application of Praxagora's guiding principle to cuisine.

14. 1042.

CONCLUSION

On the *Knights* and the *Assemblywomen*

The *Knights* and the *Assemblywomen* both depict cities which collapse the public and the private, but which do so in opposite ways.[1] In the *Knights*, Demos, the man who will only talk politics on the Pnyx,[2] or in the Assembly, is seduced into leaving the Assembly and the city for the countryside. In the *Knights*, the public is collapsed into the private, as the play's final scene suggests. Agoracritas gives to Demos Spartan peace terms represented as young women. Because women in Athens were confined to the home, women stand for the private realm, and in the *Knights* women stand for the private in a double sense. For not only do the female peace terms represent the pleasures and interests which the city strives to protect, but which the city often threatens, and which it would seem, can exist independently of the city; but the peace terms were kept hidden by Paphlagon inside his own house for his own self-interest. The female peace terms represent Paphlagon's private interest. Paphlagon's private interest is for the war to continue. The public man needs the public problem of war in order to maintain Demos' public-spiritedness, which keeps Demos from being absorbed by the private realm. In the *Knights*, the female is introduced in order to lure Demos from the polis, into the private realm. Not even a cushioned seat can make the Pnyx more appealing.

In the *Assemblywomen*, the female is introduced to de-nature the men, to give birth to a second nature, or to turn them from self-interest to the common, or public. One might say that the public is served, but the price is high. The city loses its political character. To understand this, it's helpful to refer to Aristotle. In Book I of the *Politics,*[3] Aristotle suggests that political life supplies both the highest and most comprehensive good. In other words, political life is both hierarchical and inclusive. In being inclusive, political life recognizes that citizens are more than parts but wholes. So among citizens there is political rule, which means that citizens are ruled, but rule in turn, or in part. Citizens are not just cogs in a machine. However, being a citizen does entail being ruled. Political life imposes a hierarchy which restricts our freedom. (In a modern liberal regime such as the United States the hierarchical character of political life is most visible within the corporation.)

In the *Assemblywomen*, equality is purchased at the price of hierarchy; needs are met but the city ceases to do anything but meet needs. This is what it means for political life to be reduced to body. The reason why Aristophanes chooses to depict this occurrence as the effeminization of politics is that the home is now the model. Within the home bodily needs are met through the use of craft (*techne*), and the home is the site of the family—an apolitical union. The family represents the possibility of association without aspiration or honor.

But given this account of women, how do we account for the women's takeover of the Assembly? If women are so private, why do they venture into the Assembly?[4] As the play makes clear, although the women take over the Assembly, this takeover is not possible without Praxagora, and Praxagora as a woman is the exception not the rule. While female, and embracing the "female solution" to the political problem, she is hyper-political, as Aristophanes reveals to us. After giving her rehearsal speech, a comrade asks where she learned to speak so beautifully, to which she responds that she took refuge in the Pnyx (during a period of instability?) "and then listening to the speakers I became conversant in speaking."[5] Praxagora, then, is the political female. She has been worked on by the polis, and no longer is simply a woman. As a politicized female, she is able to put the female into words. Praxagora reduces the female to a principle. So now the city can be female, or it can be run by the assemblywomen, and a man can be a woman. That we are given no reason to conclude that Blepyrus changes out of his wife's clothing turns out to be significant. Thus, in the *Assemblywomen*, even gender becomes a matter of convention. By contrast, in the *Knights*, the play closes with Agoracritus returning Demos to the peak of manhood. The *Assemblywomen* is post-political; the *Knights* pre-political. The *Assemblywomen* concludes with the end of history; the *Knights* with the state of nature, or with Demos' re-barbarization.

This distinction between the two plays manifests itself in the use of costume and names. In the *Knights*, as we move from beginning to end the characters are stripped down to their natural selves. By the end of the play, name and dress reveal instead of obscure. Thus, while at the start the demagogue is known to us only by his pseudonym (Paphlagon) and, as Aristophanes makes clear, not even his mask resembles his face,[6] at 976 this pseudonym is momentarily dropped. And, while the sausage-seller, the true son of Demos, appears to us at first in the dress of his profession, by play's end his dress changes to accord with his closeness to Demos and his democratic virtue. In Demos' last act of the play he bestows upon Agoracritus a distinctive green robe (1406), symbolizing his distinctive closeness to Demos and his amazing ingenuity in his service. His dress now corresponds to his being. Moreover, Agoracritus' name accords with his actual achievements in the play (he wins the fight in the Senate, and so he names himself Victor Senate) and with the personality he displayed growing up (Agoracritus, because he grew up disputing in the agora). And, while at the start of the play, Demos is a feeble, half-witted old man, thoroughly incapable of rule, and is dressed in rags. At the end of the play, he is young and spry, is dressed in royal attire, and is called "monarch of the Greeks" (1333). At the start of the play, democracy was a misnomer. Name and reality were at odds, because Demos did not really rule. At the end of the play, Demos is king. However, to exercise rule, Demos must leave political life and return to the countryside; nature takes precedence over conventional life, as names and costume reflect reality.

In the *Assemblywomen,*[7] the opposite move occurs. Costume and convention become more important. As noted, in the *Assemblywomen*, not only do the women dress as men, but also the men dress as women. In the hag scene, old women dress as young women. Instead of a return to nature, which we get in the *Knights*, we move away from nature. In the *Knights*, political life withers away so convention withers away. In the *Assemblywomen*, convention overcomes nature, so convention becomes all-important. That Athenian women come to rule in Athens reflects the dominance of convention.

This distinction also manifests itself with respect to sex. In the *Knights*, in keeping with the return to nature towards which the play moves, the newly rejuvenated and beautified Demos is presented with the female Spartan peace terms with whom he may satisfy his sexual desire. In the *Knights* the natural standard of beauty gets the respect it deserves. By contrast, in the *Assemblywomen*, the law forces beauty and youth to subordinate themselves to the ugly and old. In the *Assemblywomen*, a conventional standard triumphs over a natural standard.

This is not to say that the end of the *Knights* is without ugliness. For in leaving behind Athens for the countryside, Demos leaves behind justice and the institutions dedicated to it. He goes to the countryside and the private realm dressed as sumptuously as the Great King, and like the Great King he has become an object of envy.[8] Before Demos was a contemptible, pitiable old fool. He became respectable through the polis, and he knows it. Recall that he will sit nowhere but on the Pnyx. Now, his respectability has nothing to do with the polis, with justice or the law. Like the Great King or perhaps the Athenians of old, that is to say the Athenians of barbarian times,[9] his will is law. Demos' power is no longer moderated by political constraints. His absolute rule will now be directed within the private realm and for private considerations. The fact that Agoracritus presents Demos not with one woman but several reminds us of a seraglio (1388-94). I would argue that Aristophanes intends for us to think of the seraglio, for the seraglio is governed absolutely by its owner and is dedicated to satisfying his private pleasure.[10] Earlier, in an endnote, I mentioned that Demosthenes during the interview in which he attempts to lure the sausage-seller into politics makes use of terms ordinarily associated with the haughty ruler, such as a Persian captain.[11] To Demosthenes' surprise and dismay, the sausage-seller brings about a revolution in which Demosthenes' terms are quite suitable.

Just as the ending of the *Knights* is not without ugliness, the *Assemblywomen* is not without beauty. This is suggested by Praxagora's response to Blepyrus' remark that the women have been put in charge. Feigning surprise, Praxagora proclaims, "By Aphrodite, then the city will be blessed from now on" (558-9, my emphasis). Praxagora's oath to the goddess of beauty occurs at the dramatic peak of the play. For only after the women have been "informed" of the Assembly's decision can they assume power. For the women to have assumed power before this point might lead to the discovery of their scheme, that is, it might lead someone to conclude that the "pale-faced shoemakers"[12] who supported handing the city over to women were themselves women. So, one might argue that it is at this point that the new Athens is born.[13] And, at this moment the goddess whom Praxagora invokes is not Athena but Aphrodite. Is Praxagora's revolution in Aphrodite's behalf after all, despite her utter defeat in the hag scene? What is beautiful about Praxagora's new city?

Praxagora's aim is to unite the city, or to make Athens whole. The absolute unity or wholeness at which Praxagora aims requires citizens to accept being mere fractions of the whole. In an effort to make the city whole, Praxagora's Athens suppresses the particular longings of the individual, for they threaten this wholeness. Therefore, private property and eros must give way to the law. To the extent that Praxagora's plan is realized, to the extent that the city is made whole or perfectly coherent, it is a beautiful thing to behold. However, since its beauty requires the suppression of eros as is evidenced by the hag scene, it comes at the cost of individual human wholeness. In order for the city to become beautiful, individuals must give up their own idea of beauty. Since the young lovers of the hag scene resist the hags and the law, we may say that Praxagora's city is not whole yet. The citizens have not yet become thoroughly mutilated, and the city is not yet beautiful. Its wholeness would presuppose the lovers' willing compliance, or their acceptance of Praxagora's good. When this compliance is realized, Praxagora's city is truly whole, and convention is truly triumphant over nature.

So, in the *Knights* nature is restored whereas in the *Assemblywomen* nature is or is about to be overcome. This result is related to what each play is about. The nature of Demos emerges in the *Knights*, for it depicts a city in which the people rule without restraint, so nothing stands in the way of the people's nature or essence becoming manifest. Convention dominates nature in the *Assemblywomen*, because it depicts a city in which the law reigns absolutely. Human nature is forced into compliance with the law so as to ensure absolute unity. In yoking together Aristophanes' depictions of rule and law, we catch a glimpse as to why Aristophanes chose not to yoke them together but to treat each separately in the *Knights* and the *Assemblywomen*. For these two plays represent the two ends of political life, which are in conflict, but which are necessary for political life.

On the one hand, political life is natural, or teleological. As Demos' experience in the *Knights* shows, political life completes us. It is the means by which our essence comes to the fore. From this perspective, political life means aiming at virtue.[14] After the sausage-seller wins the battle of the oracles, Demos declares, "And now I entrust myself here to you to guide my old age and to re-educate me" (1098-9). As we have seen, the sausage-seller more than lives up to Demos' expectations. By the end of the play, Agoracritus has not only re-educated Demos, but has returned Demos to youth; and, the knights and their aristocratic virtue have become irrelevant, while Demos and his democratic virtue have been elevated to an exalted position.[15] By the end of the play, Demos' essence has become manifest. No polis, no growth or self-knowledge.

On the other hand, political life is for living together. Therefore, to some extent it must impose an equality on us. Citizens are equal at least with respect to the conventions which define the citizen, whatever those conventions happen to be. In the *Assemblywomen*, towards the end of the dialogue scene, Blepyrus asks, "what way of life will you make?" To which Praxagora responds, "common (*koinein*) for all" (673).[16] Without the common, the city exists in name only, and is really just a place where people pursue their own interests. If nothing is in common, there is no city.

In juxtaposing the two plays, one sees that the two ends of the city are difficult to reconcile. In the *Knights*, by the end of the play, the communal character of political life has been lost. Demos has been purified, his essence has been shown, but Demos is all that is left, and Demos is one man. In the *Assemblywomen*, the city is one house, but virtue is dispensed with for it gives rise to envy which obstructs the unity of the city. In juxtaposing the two plays, one also sees that while the ends of political life are difficult to reconcile, political life requires both. It is no accident that in both the *Knights* and the *Assemblywomen*, by the conclusion of each play the city has lost its political character. In the *Knights*, Demos will no longer sit on the Pnyx; and, in the *Assemblywomen*, Praxagora uses the hardware of the Assembly for the purpose of feeding the citizens. Although in the *Knights* and the *Assemblywomen*, Aristophanes has not shown us how rule and law may be reconciled, his plays have an important moderating effect. For they make us aware of a tension between the two ends of political life as fundamental to political life as the two ends themselves.

Notes

1. Cf. Said, "Assemblywomen," 298. "More precisely, women becoming powerful is a way of saying that the power has changed, that politics as such exist no more, and that economics has invaded everything, in the same way as the acquisition of power by a sausage merchant in the *Knights* indicates that politics has been downgraded to cooking." Although I think that both plays demonstrate the same movement, the significance of this movement in the two plays differs.

It is a commonplace observation that Aristophanes' plays collapse the public and the private. As Segal says in "The Physis of Comedy," "Aristophanic comedy characteristically reduces statecraft to housekeeping." Segal, *Oxford Readings*, 5. See also Foley, "Women." The obscenity which prevails in Attic comedy can be viewed as a manifestation of the collapse of public and private. There is perhaps no better symbol of the collapse of the public and the private than the leather *phalloi* which all male characters wear.

2. 750-1.

3. 1252a1-6.

4. One might say, that women represent the private is the very basis of the comedy. Why would assemblywomen be comical if women were not symbolic of the private? In any case, not even the masculine Praxagora can take over the city as a woman. She must do so dressed as a man. Her name may mean, active in the Agora—the public square.

5. 241-4.

6. At *Knights* 220-2, Aristophanes has Demosthenes tell the sausage-seller not to worry about Paphlagon's appearance, because none of the mask-makers had the courage to make an actual likeness of him.

7. At 339-40, an anonymous friend of Blepyrus claims to have suffered the same fate as Blepyrus, meaning he too has been forced to wear his wife's clothing.

8. The chorus declares just before the rejuvenated Demos enters:

> Oh gleaming, violet crowned and all-envied Athens, show us the monarch of Greece and this land (1329-30).

Note, the chorus declares that Athens not Demos is all-envied. However, it is Demos not Athens that Agoracritus has rejuvenated. It is Demos who is all-envied not Athens.

The chorus' failure to understand this suggests that it has been thoroughly duped by Agoracritus. The knights think he works for them, and that he will return Athens to its former self, when the knights had more power and Demos less. As Demos' response to the knights' greeting shows, however, they could not be more wrong. After the knights herald Demos' entrance (see 1333-4), Demos does not so much as acknowledge their presence, and the knights never say another word. Their non-participation in the play reflects their non-participation in Athens. It should be noted that the *Knights* is the only extant comedy with a conclusion in which the chorus figures in no way. In fact, commentators had accounted for this by assuming that our copy of the play is incomplete. For example, Dover says, "No other Aristophanic play ends without . . . a song . . . , and it is reasonably suspected that the original ending of *Knights* is lost. We would have expected a line or two of song" (*Aristophanic Comedy*, 92-3). Croiset notes "how little importance is attached to the chorus in the *denouement*. . . . Agoracritos alone prescribes the rules for Demos' future conduct; during this time the chorus does not utter a single word." He adds, "of course it may be that, as they withdrew, they gave vent to their joy in a final song that has been lost." Croiset, *Aristophanes*, 76. It seems to me, however, that the absence of a final choral ode is consistent with the argument of the play.

9. There is some similarity between Demos' dress as described by Agoracritus and the dress of the old Athenians as described by Thucydides:

> Behold the man adorned with the golden cicada, resplendent in old dress, not smelling of mussel-shells but of peace libations, anointed with myrrh (1331-2).

> [I]t is only lately that their (Athens') rich old men left off the luxury of wearing undergarments of linen, and fastening a knot of their hair with a tie of golden grasshoppers. . . . And there are many other points in which a likeness might be shown between the life of the Hellenic world of old and the barbarian of today (I.6.; Richard Crawley, trans.).

In the final scene, Demos' re-barbarization is also suggested to us when Demos declares that he will force young admirers of political rhetoric "to cease moving decrees, and to go hunting instead" (1382-3). Not speech and law but appetite and the arts that are dedicated to satisfying it shall occupy the young.

10. Cf 1253a29ff. Here Aristotle suggests that the family is barbaric unless it is part of a polis. "For just as a man is the best of the animals when completed, when separated from law and adjudication he is the worst of all."

For a revealing account of the seraglio see Montesquieu's *Persian Letters*.

11. See above, chapter 2, p. 19 and corresponding notes 12 and 13.

12. 431-3. Chremes mistakes the disguised women for pale-faced shoemakers. Evidently the women were not as well-disguised as they thought.

13. Note that immediately after Blepyrus' "revelation" the dialogue scene begins in which Praxagora makes evident her reform program.

14. Recall that in the *Assemblywomen*, Praxagora as part of her attempt to foster community makes virtue irrelevant. See chapter 7, above.

15. Although, as Strauss observes, the knights in supporting the sausage-seller have been dragged into the muck of political life, and so are knights no longer. *Socrates and Aristophanes*, 86.

16. Praxagora's response might also be translated, "common with respect to all things." In the city of the *Assemblywomen*, the common is all that matters.

BIBLIOGRAPHY

Adkins, A.W.H. *Moral Values and Political Behavior in Ancient Greece: Homer to the End of the Fifth Century*. New York: Norton, 1972.

Aquinas, Thomas. *On Kingship*, trans. Gerald Phelan. Toronto: The Pontifical Institute of Mediaeval Studies, 1949.

Aristophanes. *Assembly of Women* (*Ecclesiazusae*), trans. Robert Mayhew. New York: Prometheus Books, 1997.

Aristophanes. *Comoediae Tomus II*. Oxford: Oxford University Press, 1907.

Aristotle. *Politics*, trans. Carnes Lord. Chicago: University of Chicago Press, 1984.

Benardete, Seth. *In the Argument of the Action: Essays on Greek Poetry and Philosophy*. Chicago: University of Chicago Press, 2000.

——. *Sacred Transgressions*. South Bend, Ind.: St. Augustine's Press, 1999.

——. "On Greek Tragedy." In *Current Developments in the Arts and Sciences*, The Great Ideas Today, 1980, 102-43. Chicago: Encyclopedia Britannica, 1980.

Bloom, Allan. *Giants and Dwarfs*. New York: Simon and Schuster, 1990.

Bowie, A.M. *Aristophanes: Myth, Ritual and Comedy*. Cambridge: Cambridge University Press, 1993.

Brock, R.W. "The Double Plot in Aristophanes' Knights." *GRBS* 27 (1986): 15-27.

Butcher, S.H. *Aristotle's Theory of Poetry and Fine Art*. London: Macmillan and Co., 1923.

Casement, William. "Political Theory in Aristophanes' *Ecclesiazusae*." *J Thought* 21 (Winter 1986): 64-79.

Clay, Diskin. "The Tragic and Comic Poet of the *Symposium*." In *Essays in Ancient Greek Philosophy*, vol. 2, ed. J.P. Anton and A. Preus. Albany: State University of New York Press, 1983.

Cornford, F.M. *The Origins of Attic Comedy*. Gloucester, Mass.: Peter Smith, 1968.

Croiset, M. *Aristophanes and the Political Parties at Athens*, trans. J. Loeb. London: Macmillan, 1909.

Davies, John Kenyon. *Athenian Propertied Families, 600–300 B.C.* Oxford: Clarendon Press, 1971.

Davis, Michael. *Ancient Tragedy and the Origins of Modern Science*. Carbondale: Southern Illinois University Press, 1988.

——. *The Politics of Philosophy*. Lanham, Md.: Rowman & Littlefield, 1996.

David, E. *Aristophanes and the Athenian Society of the Early Fourth Century B.C.* The Netherlands: Mnemosyne, 1984.

De Ste. Croix, G.E.M. "The Political Outlook of Aristophanes." In *Oxford Readings in Aristophanes*, ed. Erich Segal. Oxford: Oxford University Press, 1996.

Dobbs, Darrell. "Aristotle's Anticommunism." *American Journal of Political Science* 29 (1985).

Dover, K.J. *Aristophanic Comedy*. Berkeley: University of California Press, 1972.

Edmunds, Lowell. *Cleon, Knights, and Aristophanes' Politics*. Lanham, Md.: University Press of America, 1987.

Ehrenberg, V. *The People of Aristophanes*. Cambridge, Mass.: Harvard University Press, 1951.

——. *The Greek State*. New York: W.W. Norton, 1964.

Euben, J. Peter. *The Tragedy of Political Theory: The Road Not Taken*. Princeton: Princeton University Press, 1986.

Finley, M.I. "Between Slavery and Freedom." In *Economy and Society in Ancient Greece*, ed. M.I. Finley. London: Chatto and Windus, 1981.

Flashar, Hellmut. "The Originality of Aristophanes' Last Plays." In *Oxford Readings in Aristophanes*, ed. Erich Segal. Oxford: Oxford University Press, 1996.

Foley, Helene P. "The 'Female Intruder' Reconsidered: Women in Aristophanes' *Lysistrata* and *Ecclesiazusae*." *Classical Philology* 77 (January 1982): 1-21.

Forde, Steven. "The Comic Poet, the City and the Gods: Dionysus' 'Katabasis' in the *Frogs* of Aristophanes." *Interpretation* 21, no. 3 (Spring 1994): 275-286.

Frazer, James George. *The Golden Bough*. New York: Simon and Schuster, 1998.

Friedman, Milton. *Capitalism and Freedom*. Chicago: University of Chicago Press, 1962.

Friedrich, Rainer. "Euripidaristophanizein and Nietzchesokratizein: Aristophanes, Nietzsche, and the Death of Tragedy." *Dionysius* no. 4 (December 1980): 5-36.

Gomme, A.W. "Aristophanes and Politics." *Classical Review* 52 (1938).

Guthrie, W.K.C. *Orpheus and Greek Religion*. New York: Norton, 1966.

Halliwell, Henderson, Sommerstein, and Zimmermann, eds. *Tragedy, Comedy and the Polis*. Bari: Levante Editori, 1993.

Havelock, E.A. *The Liberal Temper in Greek Politics*. New Haven: Yale University Press, 1957.

Heath, Malcolm. *Political Comedy in Aristophanes*. Gottingen: Vandenhoeck & Ruprecht, 1987.

Henderson, Jeffrey. *The Maculate Muse: Obscene Language in Attic Comedy.* New York: Oxford University Press, 1991.

Herington, C.J. *Athena Parthenos and Athena Polias.* Manchester: Manchester University Press, 1955.

Hobbes, Thomas. *Leviathan.* New York: Collier Books, 1962.

Hubbard, Thomas K. *The Mask of Comedy: Aristophanes and the Intertextual Parabasis.* Ithaca, N.Y.: University of Cornell Press, 1991.

Hugill, W.M. *Panhellenism in Aristophanes.* Chicago: University of Chicago Press, 1936.

Kennedy, G. *The Art of Persuasion in Greece.* Princeton: Princeton University Press, 1963.

Kremer, Mark. "Aristophanes' Criticism of Egalitarianism: An Interpretation of the *Assemblywomen.*" *Interpretation* 21, no. 3 (Spring 1994): 261-274.

Lindblom, Charles E. *Politics and Markets.* New York: Basic Books, 1977.

Linforth, I. *The Arts of Orpheus.* Berkeley: University of California Press, 1941.

Jaeger, W. *Demosthenes.* Berkeley: University of California Press, 1938.

Jones, A.H.M. *Athenian Democracy.* Baltimore: Johns Hopkins University Press, 1986.

MacDowell, Douglas M. *Aristophanes and Athens: An Introduction to the Plays.* Oxford: Oxford University Press, 1995.

Montesquieu. *Persian Letters*, trans. C.J. Betts. New York: Penguin Books, 1993.

Murphy, C.T. "Aristophanes and the Art of Rhetoric." *Harvard Studies in Classical Philology* 49 (1938).

Murray, Gilbert. *Aristophanes: A Study.* New York: Oxford University Press, 1933.

Mylonas, G.E. *Eleusis and the Eleusinian Mysteries.* Princeton: Princeton University Press, 1962.

Neil, Robert A. *The Knights of Aristophanes.* London: Cambridge University Press, 1909.

Nichols, Mary. Socrates and the Political Community: an Ancient Debate. Albany, N.Y.: State University Press of New York, 1987.

——. *Citizens and Statesmen.* Lanham, Md.: Rowman & Littlefield, 1992.

Nilsson, M.P. *Greek Popular Religion.* New York: Columbia University Press, 1940.

Norwood, G. *Greek Comedy.* Boston: J.W. Luce & Co., Inc., 1932.

——. "The Babylonians of Aristophanes." *Classical Philology* 25 (1930): 1-10.

Park, H.W. *Festivals of the Athenians.* London: Thames and Hudson, 1977.

Pickard-Cambridge, A. *Dithyramb, Tragedy, Comedy.* Oxford: Clarendon Press, 1927.

Plato. *Republic*, trans. Allan Bloom. New York: Basic Books, 1968.

———. *Symposium*, trans. Seth Benardete. Chicago: University of Chicago Press, 2001.

——. *Minos*, trans. Seth Benardete, unpublished.

——. *Apology*, in Plato I, Loeb Classical Library. Cambridge, Mass.: Harvard University Press, 1990.

Plutarch. *The Lives of the Noble Grecians and Romans*, trans. John Dryden. New York: Modern Library, 1992.

Reynolds, L.D., and Wilson, N.G. *Scribes and Scholars: A Guide to the Transmission of Greek and Latin Literature*. Oxford: Oxford University Press, 1968.

Rogers, B.B. *Aristophanes' Comedies*. London: Bell, 1902.

Rothwell, Kenneth Sprague. *Politics and Persuasion in Aristophanes' Ecclesiazusae*. New York: E.J. Brill, 1990.

Rousseau, Jean-Jacques. *Emile*, trans. Allan Bloom. New York: Basic Books, 1979.

——. *On the Social Contract*, trans. Donald Cress. Indianapolis: Hackett Publishing Co., 1987.

Russo, Carlo Ferdinando. *Aristophanes, an Author for the Stage*. London: Routledge, 1994.

Said, Suzanne. "The *Assemblywomen*: Women, Economy and Politics." In *Oxford Readings in Aristophanes*, ed. Erich Segal. Oxford: Oxford University Press, 1996.

Salman, Charles. "The Wisdom of Plato's Aristophanes." *Interpretation* (Winter 1990-91): 233-250.

Sandel, Michael, ed. *Liberalism and its Critics*. New York: New York University Press, 1984.

Saxonhouse, Arlene. *The Fear of Diversity*. Chicago: University of Chicago Press, 1992.

——. "The Net of Hephaestus: Aristophanes' Speech in Plato's Symposium." *Interpretation* 13 (January 1985): 15-32.

Segal. C.P. "The Character and Cults of Dionysus and the Unity of the *Frogs*." *Harvard Studies in Classical Philology* 65 (1961).

Segal, Erich. *Oxford Readings in Aristophanes*, ed. Erich Segal. Oxford: Oxford University Press, 1996.

Silk, M.S. "The Autonomy of Comedy." *Comparative Criticism* 10 (1988): 3-31.

——. "Aristophanes as a Lyric Poet." *Yale Classical Studies* 26 (1980): 99-151.

Sommerstein, Alan H. *Aristophanes: Knights*. Wilts: Aris & Phillips, Ltd., 1981.

Sophocles, *Antigone*, in *Sophocles II*. Loeb Classical Library. Cambridge, Mass.: Harvard University Press, 1994.

Starkie, W.J.M. *The Aeharnians of Aristophanes*. London: Macmillan and Co., 1909.

Storing, Herbert, ed. *The Anti-Federalist, An Abridgement* by Murray Dry. Chicago: University of Chicago Press, 1981.

Strauss, Leo. *Socrates and Aristophanes*. Chicago: University of Chicago Press, 1966.

——. *The City and Man*. Chicago: University of Chicago Press, 1964.

Sutton, Dana Ferrin. *Ancient Comedy: The War of the Generations*. New York: Twayne Publishers, 1993.

——. *Self and Society in Aristophanes*. Washington, D.C.: University Press of America, 1980.

Taaffe, Lauren K. *Aristophanes and Women*. London: Routledge, 1993.

Taplin, Oliver. "Fifth-Century Tragedy and Comedy." In *Oxford Readings in Aristophanes*, ed. Erich Segal. Oxford: Oxford University Press, 1996.

Thucydides. *The History of the Peloponnesian War*, trans. Richard Crawley. London: Everyman's Library Edition, 1993.

Ussher, R.G. *Aristophanes*. Oxford: Clarendon Press, 1979.

——. *Aristophanes: Ecclesiazusae*. Oxford: Oxford University Press, 1973.

Whitman, Cedric. *Aristophanes and the Comic Hero*. Cambridge, Mass.: Harvard University Press, 1964.

Wycherley, R.E. "Aristophanes and Euripides." *Greece and Rome* 15 (1946).

Xenophon. *Hiero*. In *Xenophon: Scripta Minora*, ed. E. Capps, T.E. Page, W.H.D. Rouse. New York: G.P. Putnam's Sons, 1925.

——. *The Polity of the Athenians*. In *Scripta Minora*, ed. E.C. Marchant. Cambridge: Harvard University Press, 1968.

Zimmermann, Bernhard. "The *Parodoi* of the Aristophanic Comedies." In *Oxford Readings in Aristophanes*, ed. Erich Segal. Oxford: Oxford University Press, 1996.

INDEX

ABOUT THE AUTHOR

Ken De Luca teaches courses in Western Culture and Political Science at Hampden-Sydney College. He also has taught at Fordham University, Assumption College and the College of the Holy Cross. He is the author of essays on Plato, Sophocles, Shakespeare, and Machiavelli.